GHOSTS
and Legends
of the
Broads

Simon Peters

LUCAS BOOKS

GHOSTS

and Legends
of the
Broads

Simon Peters

First Published 2007
by Lucas Books
ISBN-13 9781903797-79-2

©Copyright Simon Peters

Printed in the UK by Printwright, Ipswich

Contents

What is a Ghost?

This is a book primarily about ghosts, ghost stories and old legends. Mixed in the brew are some of the old superstitions people used to believe long ago and even a few old remedies and snippets of amusing folklore. Some of the ghost stories are ones I have been told when I lived in and travelled around Broadland, and, as far as I know, they are published here for the first time. Some of the other tales have been around for many years and they have been told and retold time and time again. One or two of the stories tell of ghosts that I have encountered. Or, perhaps, regarding that last category, I should say that within these pages you will find some stories about ghosts that I think I have encountered.

I've loved listening to spooky stories for as long I can remember. Indeed, my Victorian grandfather took great delight in telling me scary tales by the light of a flickering gas lamp while his big black boots were warming by the fire. He was a master storyteller and his words painted pictures of greater colour and detail in my young imagination than any image an artist could create with brush and oils, or any photographer might hope to achieve with a camera.

Grandfather's words would hold me enthralled. His power to conjure images into my mind's eye never failed. Even when he recounted one of his tales for the twentieth time, to me it was like hearing it for the very first time. Masterfully and deliberately he would ratchet up the suspense as only a gifted storyteller can, and then, seeing the agony of fearful anticipation building within the eyes of his young listener, he would cause the climax of his tale to burst over me with the force of a waterfall.

Then there would be a deep and total silence; a silence that was broken only by the purring whisper of the gas mantle.

Grandfather would chuckle softly, give a knowing wink, and smack the bowl of his pipe into the palm of his hand. Then, exactly on cue, grandmother would enter the room and declare, 'Have you been telling young Simon one of your silly stories again?' Grandfather would wink again and smile innocently as the small grey-haired lady reached forward to turn up the gas lamp. Immediately all the threatening shadows that had been closing in upon me were banished to the distant corners of the room. 'Come on, it's bedtime,' she would command, and suddenly I was a child back in the real world again.

I suppose it's fair to say that the telling and retelling of tales – and listening to them over and over again – must be one of the oldest pleasures we human beings have enjoyed. And my bet is that back in the days when families and friends gathered around the fire at night, many of the tales that were told were about ghosts and spirits and the unseen things that go bump in the night. Or to put it more succinctly, happenings that have no easy or obvious explanation. And before we dismiss many of the old tales let us bear in mind that there may be a nugget of truth at the core of many an ancient fable.

Without a doubt, there are some days – or rather nights – that are better suited than others for telling spooky tales. At least that has been my experience. Some days of the year seem to have a special 'atmosphere'. Hallowe'en, and the twelve days of Christmastide, particularly Twelfth Night, are among the best. So too are the longest and shortest days of the year [June 21 and December 22], as well as Candlemas Night [February 2], and the eves [or vigils] of St Agnes [January 20], St Valentine [February 13] St Mark [April 24], May Day, Lammas [July 31], St Catherine [November 24] and St Thomas [December 20].

What is a Ghost?

Perhaps it should be no surprise that while these days are remarkably well-suited for telling ghost stories, according to folklore they are also particularly good for young lovers to get predictions about the future direction of their love lives.

Undoubtedly the very best 'atmosphere' for listening to spooky tales comes when a dozen or so men and women, boys and girls, gather around a roaring fire on a dark and stormy winter's night. Then minds are more easily opened and imaginations more easily stimulated. Certainly that was true in the days when the flames of a log fire and the soft, flickering light of two or three candles provided the only illumination. Then all one's instincts seem sharper and one's senses are more receptive. And if a jug of hot punch is close to hand, so much the better. Try it for yourself.

And if after reading this book you decide to do a little ghost-hunting yourself, I suggest that you take along a notebook and a pencil, a watch, a good torch, and perhaps a camera. You might get lucky, but be warned, ghosts are notoriously camera-shy. As for all the other paraphernalia to record any sudden fluctuations in temperature, pressure or humidity, or to detect vibrations or high-pitched noises, don't bother. If there's a ghost around you'll soon know about it. I remember having a long silent laugh when I heard it seriously suggested that a wind chime and a tin of talcum powder were essential pieces of kit for any ghost-hunter.

Down the years I have never lost my appetite for tales of ghosts and strange hauntings. I have read plenty of ghost stories, some good, some bad, and many I regret to say that have been concocted by authors sitting at a typewriter or a computer many miles from the site of the alleged haunting. Down the years many people have been willing to share with me their experiences of ghosts and unexplained happenings. I thank them all. Through them I have become acquainted and sometimes re-acquainted with dozens of ghosts old and not-so-old, and this book is my opportunity to pass on some of their tales to you.

As you will see, some of the ghosts were helpful, and some were hideous; some were protective and some were pitiable. But in each and every case it seems that they wanted their supernatural existence to be known and their tale to be told.

So what is a ghost and why do they seem to haunt people and places? I suppose for most people the definition of a ghost is the spirit of a person or animal now dead. When someone dies we say they have 'given up the ghost'. Ghosts exist - or are presumed to exist - because for centuries religion has taught us that our earthly life is followed by an afterlife or another existence in some form or another. So a ghost is a spirit existing in a state after the death of the physical body and before full entry into the realm of the dead. A ghost is a spirit entity that manifests itself in our world, our reality, while it still occupies a time and space between this world and the next, between this existence and the next. Because it is

between states it usually appears to us as something insubstantial, something unreal.

We sometimes use words taken from other languages to describe much the same thing – spook comes from Dutch, spectre from Latin, phantasm from Greek. We also speak of apparition, phantom, shade, and wraith. Strictly speaking a wraith is an apparition that appears before death, not after.

So why do ghosts appear? You can get a lot of answers to that question. Here are some of the reasons that have been put forward. It would not surprise me one little bit if you had a chuckle at some of them.

Ghosts appear because they are dead but they don't know it. Although they are dead they still feel very much 'alive' so they look for a new home and when they settle on a place that becomes a 'haunted' place.

They don't know where to go in their spirit form.

In life they were bad and broke the law so they remain earthbound to avoid going to the punishment that awaits them in Hell.

They have come back to accompany another ghost that is reluctant to depart.

They have come back to warn a relative or loved one of danger.

They are afraid of coming face to face in the afterlife with someone they were in conflict with in life. This could include an ex-wife or ex-husband.

If a victim of murder or another crime they delay their departure from this world until they have seen justice done.

They stay where they are because they feel undeserving of a place in Heaven.

They prefer what this world has to offer above the unknown delights of the next.

They are afraid of losing their status, importance and

wealth in the next world.

Rather bizarrely I have seen it suggested that those who die from an addiction refuse to move on because they prefer to remain and seek to occupy another body so that they might continue their destructive habit in this world.

Ghostly appearances are caused by a distortion of Time or an irregularity in the Earth's magnetic field. Alternatively they are caused by a distortion of the power of ley lines or a sudden release of energy from deep within the Earth's core.

Just as you can find many reasons to explain why ghosts appear, so you can find plenty of theories that seek to divide ghosts and hauntings into different categories. Not all ghosts manifest themselves visually. Some make their presence known by smells or noises such as tapping and knocking on walls and doors when no one is to be seen. More disturbing can be the sound of footsteps or breathing or distorted voices. Sometimes a ghost may make its presence known by moving items from one room to another or by making things fall off shelves or by turning electrical equipment on and off. And there can be hauntings in which people – or rather some people - detect a 'presence' or a 'force'.

Many of the old ghost stories revolve around a certain date in the calendar. These are often called 'anniversary hauntings' and they have been explained as being the re-enactment of the original event. One suggestion is that if the original event was particularly dramatic and traumatic then the energy that was generated in that conflict or crime was absorbed and stored within the environment where it happened. A replay is triggered when the anniversary comes round. Another type of haunting is that caused by a ghost returning to our world in an attempt to communicate with someone.

What is a Ghost?

For those of a nervous disposition there is the comfort of the old belief that ghosts must disappear at cock-crow. In support of this let me quote Henry Bourne, a Cambridge antiquarian and man of the Church who lived three hundred years and more ago. He wrote, 'There is a tradition among the common people that at the Cock-crowing the Mid-night spirits forsake these lower regions, and go to their proper places. Hence it is that in the country villages, where the way of life requires more early labour, the inhabitants always go cheerfully to work at that time; whereas if they are called abroad sooner, they are apt to imagine everything they see or hear to be a wandering Ghost.' It was a notion Shakespeare made use of when the ghost of Hamlet's father appeared. Henry Bourne attributed the mandatory departure of spirits when the cock started crowing to religious reasons.

I've heard it said that the reason many church steeples were topped with 'weather cocks' [weather vanes in the shape of a cock] was to remind the spirits of the night to depart and the living to get up and get busy. These days the daily round of those of us who live in villages is much the same as people everywhere else. In the days before clocks and watches were everywhere days were divided into thirteen parts – 1 After midnight, 2 Cock crow, 3 The space between Cock-crow and break of day, 4 The Dawn of the Morning, 5 Morning, 6 Noon, 7 Afternoon, 8 Sunset, 9 Twilight, 10 Evening, 11 Candle-time, 12 Bed-time, 13 The Dead of the Night. The ghosts came out in 'the Dead of the Night'. [Another more uncharitable explanation for the popularity of 'weather cocks' has been offered and it's a very old one too. It's this - weather cocks were put up in abundance to ridicule the French.]

There was another way of banishing spirits. Long ago it was believed that spirits hated the sound of church bells so when an individual was close to death a bell would be rung. It was called the passing-bell or soul-bell and it was tolled just before the death of the individual, not after. Francis Grose, another 18th century antiquary wrote, 'The passing bell was anciently rung for two purposes; one to bespeak the prayers of all good Christians for a soul just departing; the other to drive away the evil spirits who stood at the bed's foot and about the house, ready to seize their prey, or at least to molest and terrify the soul in its passage: but by the ringing of that bell (for evil spirits are much afraid of bells) they were kept aloof; and the soul, like a hunted hare, gained the start, or had what is by sportsmen called law.'

Rich people would pay to have the biggest bell tolled because it was louder and would force the evil spirits to retreat even further to be beyond its tones and that gave the departing soul an even better start.

How things have changed!

Way back in 1743 a poem written in blank verse was published. It was called 'The Grave' and was by a Scottish church minister called Robert Blair who was in his 40s. It proved to be a huge success. Here are a few lines that describe perfectly the awe and scary dread in which churchyards were once held by youngsters of a parish. And it offers the classic image of the supposedly haunted churchyard. Those of you who are old enough to remember taking a short cut through the local churchyard on the way home from cubs or youth club on a dark November night for 'a dare' will know what I mean.

Oft in the lone churchyard at night I've seen,
By glimpse of moonshine, chequering thro' the trees,
The schoolboy, with his satchel in his hand,
Whistling aloud to bear his courage up.
And lightly tripping o'er the long flat stones

What is a Ghost?

(With nettles skirted, and with moss o'ergrown,)
That tell in homely phrase who lie below.
Sudden he starts! And hears, or thinks he hears,
The sound of something purring at his heels:
Full fast he flies, and dare not look behind him,
Till, out of breath, he overtakes his fellows;
Who gather round, and wonder at the tale
Of horrid apparition, tall and ghastly,
That walks at dead of night, or takes his hand
O'er some new open'd grave; and (strange to tell!)
Vanishes at crowing of the cock.

Running through a graveyard at night with a thumping, pumping heart is something lads from more innocent times may well recall. The fear of rounding a corner and being confronted by a spook all white and scary was real enough if you were on your own. Another ritual that was regularly carried out in the old days at Christmas, Easter and Whitsuntide probably didn't help the over-imaginative night-walker. In some places they used to limewash the stones that marked the head and foot of a grave. Imagine the effect by moonlight.

Of course there are plenty of people who will dismiss all tales of ghosts and hauntings as nonsense and old wives' tales. 'It's all in the mind', they'll say. Indeed, most of us who have never seen a ghost have our own ideas of what a ghostly apparition should look like, and those preconceptions are only heightened by the environment, the atmosphere and the time of day. As Henry Bourne said, 'Night, indeed, by its awfulness and horror, naturally inclines the mind of man to these reflections, which are much heightened by the legendary stories of nurses and old women.'

The Ghost that Killed a King

Did you know that a king of England was killed by a ghost? Yes, that's right. A king of England was killed stone dead by a ghost. The story is recorded in the old chronicles and those old chronicles were written by holy monks, so it must be true!

And what has it got to do with the land of the Broads? Well, that killing of a king by a ghost from the past was the culmination of a tale of treachery, murder and mayhem that had been set in motion by a few minutes of freakishly violent weather hundreds of miles from Norfolk.

It had all begun when an ill-wind from the north-east ruined a Viking's day by sweeping him and his little boat far out into the empty grey wastes of the North Sea until, at last, he and his faithful hound were deposited more dead than alive on the banks of the River Yare at Reedham. It is a story in which the tentacles of revenge, retribution and, some would say, holy justice reach down through the years with surprising results.

But before I tell you about that let me tell you a little more about the king who was killed by a spear-wielding spook that only he could see. In one version of the story he was sitting on his horse surrounded by his army when he saw the ghost coming straight toward him. 'Help! Help me!' screamed the king. His soldiers stood by helpless and bewildered. 'He's coming to kill me!' bellowed their king as the spectre marched purposefully onward with a shining spear held firmly in its right hand. But within the dense ranks of his soldiers there was not a single warrior who could see the cause of their king's desperate cries. The king was the only living being whose eyes could see the advancing spectre.

The Ghost that Killed a King

'Help me! Save me! He's coming to slay me!' yelled the terrified monarch in tones that were ever more frantic, every more fearful. But all his cries were in vain. None but he could see the avenging spirit, and he was just as helpless as were all those warriors around him to whom the danger remained bafflingly invisible. The blood drained from the living king's face as the ghost halted in front of him and raised the razor-sharp spear high above its head. Then, with a single stroke, the weapon was thrust clean through the body of the terrified and quivering king. The soldiers looked on helplessly as their king fell mortally wounded from his horse with a despairing cry of fear spilling from his quivering lips.

The monks who recorded this story many centuries ago did not agree on every detail, but they did agree about one thing and that was that the stricken king died a most wretched death. Though his body was wracked by pain, somehow he clung on to life through the fading light of that winter afternoon. Then, as the last streaks of twilight drained from the distant horizon, his spirit finally surrendered to death, and, in the words of the monks who compiled the old chronicles, 'the king died most miserably'. The scene of that fearful incident was Gainsborough in Lincolnshire and it happened around a thousand years ago on Wednesday, February 3, 1014.

I am going to make you wait a little longer before I tell you the identities of that ghost and that unfortunate king because it's time to go back to the beginning of the tale, back to the day when a freak squall of wind and hail and rain three hundred miles from the East Anglian coast sent a small boat on a hazardous voyage that ended at Reedham. In that boat was another king, a king who, like the king who was killed by the ghost, was a king with plenty of Viking blood in his veins.

Today you can get to the small riverside community of

Reedham by car, by train, by ferry, or by sailing along the usually placid waters of the River Yare. The river and a landscape of flat marshlands lie to the east, south and west of the village, and seven miles away to the east, as the crow flies, is the North Sea. But some two thousand years ago the waters of the North Sea were much closer. Indeed two thousand years ago the spot where Reedham now stands was at the edge of the sea looking out across a large estuary of mud flats and open water. But for year after year the slow and inexorable actions of the shifting tides and the powerful currents had been slowly reshaping the coastline.

Gradually the island of Flegg was joined to the mainland and a long finger of sand and shingle was formed forcing the River Yare to turn southward in its relentless search for the sea. More centuries passed and some men and women built their homes on the dunes near the mouth of the Yare and that was how the town of Great Yarmouth was born.

About a thousand years ago King William the Conqueror, the Abbot of St Benet of Holm and a Norman warrior called Richard shared the ownership of Reedham. The manor was said to be one league and three furlongs long and half a league wide. For those of you who are unfamiliar with the old measurements, a league is three miles and a furlong [or long furrow] is 220 yards or a little over 200 metres, and there are eight furlongs in a mile.

On the eve of the First World War the ancient parish of Reedham was measured at 3,321 acres with some of those acres designated as tidal and foreshore. That was a time when Reedham had its own steam powered sawmill and flourmill, limekiln, a foundry, a brickworks, and an estate noted for its heronry. And among the tradesmen living and working in the village were a bootmaker, a shoemaker, a hoop and hurdle maker, grocers, drapers, dressmaker and tailors as well as butchers, blacksmiths, farmers, marshmen, cowkeepers, boat builder, wherry owner and a miller. It was a self-sufficient little world in which the vicar had his own gardener, the school was attended by more than two hundred children, and on Sundays the schoolmaster played the church organ. But that peaceful, industrious and sometimes elegant world, like the more brutal worlds that had been inhabited by William the Conqueror and the Abbot of St Benet's and Ragnar Lothbrok, has long since passed away into history.

At this point you are probably thinking, 'Wait a minute. Who is this Ragnar Lothbrok who has suddenly popped up, and what has he got to do with the story of a king who was killed by a ghost?'

Ragnar was a Viking chieftain – some say he was king of Denmark and Sweden for a few years – and his life was full of deeds of blood and thunder, fire and fury. According to one of the old chronicles he once led a fleet of dragon ships up the River Seine to plunder Paris. In another ancient Norse saga he is said to have killed a dragon. Certainly some amazing tales have become attached to his name so it is fair to say that Ragnar was not the sort of character who would have settled down to the well-ordered and law-abiding life of a farmer, grocer or church organist in Reedham in Edwardian England.

Yes, Ragnar had a fearsome reputation among both his friends and his foes – and he certainly made plenty of foes during his lifetime. But it was the way that he was despatched to join his Viking ancestors in Valhalla that brought down a storm of terrible retribution upon the people of Reedham, and much of the rest of England too. But before we get to that let me pause just long enough to tell that there is another version of how Ragnar met his end. It is claimed that he was captured by one of his many enemies, the King of Northumberland, who had him thrown into a pit of snakes. At this point you might be thinking to yourself that some of this is beginning to sound a little familiar. You may even be conjuring up in your mind the picture of a very hairy and very shaggy Viking shouting 'Odin!' as he leaps sword in hand into a pit of snarling and ravenous wolves. Well, if that is the picture that is forming in your mind it is probably in glorious Technicolor and the hairy Viking may well look remarkably like the famous Hollywood actor of the 1950s and 1960s, Ernest Borgnine.

Yes, a version of the story of Ragnar was woven into the plot of the 1958 blood and thunder action film 'The Vikings' which starred Kirk Douglas, Tony Curtis, Janet Leigh and, of course, Ernest Borgnine as the bearded and shaggy Ragnar Lothbrok. Lothbrok [or Lodbrog] was Ragnar's nickname. It meant 'shaggy breeches'. But let us now get back to the story of Ragnar as it has been told in Reedham for many centuries.

One fine Spring day Ragnar was out wildfowling with his favourite hawk on his arm and his faithful hound trotting close beside his horse. As he and his companions followed the coastal path, offshore a flotilla of small boats kept pace with the hunters. The sport was good and time after time Ragnar's hawk took flight to bring down its prey. Ragnar and his companions had almost had their fill of sport when he sent his hawk climbing high into the sky one last time. The hunters cheered and laughed among themselves as the bird dived like a falling arrow before stabbing its dagger-like talons into its prey. But this time there was uncommon courage in the victim bird and together hawk and wildfowl fell out of the sky locked together in a struggling, writhing, screeching ball of blood and feathers.

Ragnar was a man of his times - rough, tough and thoroughly uncultured. That's why other men of violence followed him though few of them trusted him. Ragnar was the sort of man who valued his hawk and his hound more than most other things in the world including any man, woman, or pile of gold. When he saw his favourite hawk fall into the sea, Ragnar immediately dismounted, jumped into one of the fleet of small boats and tongue-lashed the oarsmen into pulling as hard as they could to the rescue of his prized hawk. The other small boats manned by warriors, nobles and hunters also turned away from the shore in search of their king's hawk. Indeed, so intent were they all on pleasing their leader that neither they nor their king noticed the threatening mass of towering black clouds that were gathering ominously around them.

Suddenly a violent squall burst upon them. First it lashed them with ice-cold rain that quickly turned to sleet and hail. In no more than a few moments the placid blue sea was transformed into a cauldron of surging black and white water. A powerful wind from the north-east fell upon them like some unseen demon intent upon capsizing each and every boat and throwing them all into that angry sea of white-topped waves as high as houses.

Ragnar and his crew of four oarsmen fought to keep their tiny craft afloat with every last ounce of their strength and with every last instinct of men skilled in the ways of ships and the sea. But the sea and the wind and the driving sleet and rain were treacherous and unforgiving enemies. For a few moments the elements relented and Ragnar and his crewmen panted on the cold air, wiped the salty spray from their faces and relaxed their holds on the ropes and the oars.

For most of them it was a fatal mistake. Within seconds the fury of the wind and the sea burst over them again with renewed violence and vigour. The little boat was tossed into an uncontrollable spin like a dry leaf caught by a winter gale. The other boats vanished from sight as one after the other the oarsmen were sent tumbling into the sea, the shriek of the numbing wind stifling their piteous and lamentable cries as they disappeared beneath the deep and impenetrable blackness of the waves.

Desperately Ragnar forced his frozen hands to grasp again at a rope and lash his exhausted body to the stub of the broken mast. He pulled his hound close to his chest and shouted at his god Thor, the lord of thunder and lightning, to chase the storm away.

Perhaps Thor the Thunderer gave ear to Ragnar's pagan prayers because gradually the power of the wind abated and no more did the waves threaten to overwhelm the little boat. Slowly the clouds cleared and the sea fell into a gentle calm. But Ragnar's ordeal was far from over. Indeed, it had just begun.

He stretched his sea-soaked limbs and body as he attempted to rub some warmth into his aching arms and legs. He grabbed hold of the stub of the mast and pulled himself onto his feet. His eyes searched the horizon in every direction but he saw only an empty sea and an empty sky. He and his faithful hound were alone, surrounded only by the cold grey wastes of the North Sea.

Night followed day and day followed night. Hunger and thirst began to torment him and many times did Ragnar look down at the limp body of the dog that lay in the bottom of the boat. Once or twice his right hand felt for the knife in his belt but each time the hound rolled his eyes and Ragnar pulled his hand away from the blade. His strong Viking will was still the master of his actions.

How many days and nights they drifted together across that empty sea no one knows. Certainly Ragnar never knew for sure. He tried to carve one notch into the gunwale for each day and night that he remained alive, but after five days – or was it seven or eight, or ten or twenty? - he had no strength left to raise his knife. Then his mind must have slipped into unconsciousness because he felt nothing when the little boat gently nosed its way into a curtain of tall and whispering reeds. And it was there that he was found with his eyes closed, his lips parched, his breathing almost undetectable, and his stiff cold fingers gripping the motionless body of a hound that appeared to be as lifeless as its master.

Ragnar was a violent and a cunning man. He was also a lucky man. Incredibly, he had survived a voyage of many hundreds of miles in an open boat sustained only by raw fish and rainwater. Perhaps even more fortunately for him, he and his little boat had come to rest on a friendly shore. How different would have been the history of England if the men who found him had merely cut his throat for the rings that he wore on his fingers and the coins that were in his purse, and then kicked the little boat with its corpse out into the grip of a retreating tide.

But they didn't. The man they found was obviously a man of status and wealth. So instead of committing murder for short-term gain they chose the path of compassion and charity in the hope of an even more lucrative reward. They reasoned that the possibility of two rewards and the thanks of a king were to be much preferred to murderers' instant gold and the very real possibility of a noose about their necks. The land where Ragnar's journey ended was the small Anglo-Saxon kingdom of East Anglia which was then ruled by a young king of noble character by the name of Edmund. Opinion about Edmund's origins vary – some say he was born in Germany – but whatever the truth of it is he was a young man destined to leave an indelible mark on history, even to the extent of becoming the patron saint of England. And there are many people today who think that Edmund should be restored to that position in place of the supposed dragon-slayer St George. But back to the tale of Ragnar the Viking.

Ragnar and his hound were lifted from the tiny boat, placed on a cart and taken to King Edmund's hall at Reedham. Again Ragnar's luck was in because Edmund happened to be in Reedham and he gave orders that the wild man from the sea should be cared for in the hope that his health would be soon restored. No doubt Edmund also prayed for the recovery of his mysterious foreign 'guest' because this young king was an eager, pious and thoroughly committed supporter of Christianity, a religion which, in the mid-ninth century, was still relatively new among his countrymen. Indeed, the churches, monks and monasteries of this young faith were coming under increasingly frequent attack by heathen Vikings from across the seas.

Time passed and Ragnar regained his strength and, much to the delight of his host, his guest's appetite for the hunt returned undiminished. It was a passion they shared although, it must be said, in all else their characters were as different as it was possible to be – one a king ever mindful of his duties to his people and his faith, and the other a cunning, rough, tough unprincipled rogue. No doubt Ragnar kept the less attractive aspects of his character well hidden from the trusting young king.

But there was one man among Edmund's close companions who developed an ever-deepening hatred for the stranger from the sea. His name was Bern and he was the East Anglian king's chief huntsman. The heathen Ragnar seemed to have the luck of the Devil's when they were out hunting, and day after day his knowledge and skill earned ever more extravagant praise and admiration from the young king.

Bern's jealousy burned ever fiercer until, one day when the king was engaged on other matters, Bern challenged Ragnar to a private duel of their hunting skills. Boar, wildfowl, deer and wolf would be their prey. Bern knew it was a challenge the proud Viking would not resist. And so it proved. And Bern also knew that for him the fowls of the air and the beasts of the forest would not be his only victims that day.

The two men left the king's hall at Reedham early that morning. Ragnar was keenly aware of Bern's jealousy and hatred, and Bern could taste the Viking's unspoken scorn. Indeed the Viking's contempt for Bern was so great, and his arrogant delight in his own skills so total that he made two mistakes that day. The first was that together they had ridden half a league in near total silence before Ragnar realised that his hound was not loping alongside his horse but was back at Reedham chained outside the hall.

Ragnar's second mistake came when the sun was high in the sky at noon. Bern muttered something about seeking the shade beneath the trees of a lonely copse where they might refresh themselves with food and drink from their saddlebags. Ragnar smiled in agreement and together they dismounted. But as they did so Ragnar's overflowing contempt for his companion dulled the caution that he had shown until that very minute. And suddenly it was too late.

He felt a strong hand grip him across his mouth and begin to pull him backward. Then he saw another hand flash past his eyes. One moment more and he felt the point of a hunting knife slice its way through his flesh and deep down into his vitals. Six, seven, eight times more the hand and the cold steel-grey blade flashed back and forth across Ragnar's narrow window of vision. Desperately he grabbed at the hand that held the knife. He tore at it. He fought with it. But the sharp-edged blade cut through the leather of his gloves. He felt a pulsing tide of blood – a pulsing tide of his own warm blood – flowing from the gashed and deep-sliced flesh that had been his hands. He clawed at the hand in vain. His assailant pulled the blade clear of the remains of Ragnar's hands and stabbed again his body. With each downward stroke the Viking felt the blade bite deeper and deeper into his body. He felt power drain from his body with each new pumping outflow of his blood. The picture of sky and trees that he could see grew dimmer and darker as did his sight of the stabbing hand and blade until, at last, cold uncaring Death wiped all vision from his eyes and all feeling from his body. Ragnar was dead. As dead as an animal speared or shot with arrows in a hunt. Bern's work was done.

That night, as they feasted in the king's hall, Bern was once again the laughing hard-drinking companion of old. The sullen and silent disposition that had hung over him during Ragnar's presence was gone. Everyone noticed and applauded the hunter's change of personality. And he, confident that there had been no witnesses to the murder, revelled again in the praise and approval that was showered upon him.

But Bern's confidence caused him to dismiss from his mind the fact that there was one witness – or more accurately, there was one witness that would soon appear to repeatedly howl the huntsman's guilt. That witness was Ragnar's hound.

The animal was chained up outside the hall and refused all food and drink that was brought to it. Time and again it pulled against the collar and chain in apparently vain endeavours to release itself. And whenever Bern came near the dog would suddenly leap up and growl in low and intimidating tones through bared teeth. Such was the dog's obvious hostility that many a time Bern wished he had cut the dog's throat or pinned it to the ground with a hunting spear.

With each passing day Edmund and his nobles became more and more convinced that the Viking's absence was no accident and Bern began to feel a wall of whispered suspicions building up around him. But he comforted himself with the knowledge that every search had failed to find a body and thus his guilt could only be hinted at. Yes, indeed he had returned that day with his cloak and tunic seemingly washed in blood. But was that to be considered unusual for a hunter who had enjoyed good sport that day?

Then Ragnar's hound broke loose. How no one knew. One night it was still there, crouching menacingly at the end of its restraining chain. By dawn it was gone. And soon King Edmund and his companions became witnesses to the most remarkable and unusual behaviour they had ever seen displayed by a hunting dog. Each night as they celebrated another successful hunt or were regaled over their cups of wine with favourite old tales, the hound would silently enter the hall unseen, and then, with a heart-stopping howl, it would burst from its hiding place and seek to bury its fangs in Bern's throat.

It was a situation that could not be allowed to continue, and as the days passed the suspicions of Edmund and his nobles grew ever stronger. Repeatedly Bern was questioned about the Viking's fate and repeatedly he denied any involvement in or knowledge of Ragnar's sudden and uncharacteristic disappearance. The hound ceased to seek out Bern and life at Edmund's court slowly returned to the more sober and pious routine that had existed before Ragnar's appearance.

Then came the news that changed everything. The body of a grey-haired hunting hound had been found in a small lonely wood a league or so to the north and east of Reedham. The body of the dog lay over the body of a man that had been hastily buried in a shallow grave. The dead man was Ragnar and in his mutilated hands was a scrap of bloodied cloth from the sleeve of a tunic. There was enough of it to be recognised.

It was Bern's.

Justice was swift. Bern was bundled into the little boat that had carried Ragnar across the North Sea. One stale loaf of bread was tossed into the boat after him. The mooring line was cut and the tiny craft kicked out into the embrace of the river's strong flow. It had been timed to coincide with the swift retreat of the tide and soon Bern found himself drifting further and further away from land.

Sometimes a stroke of good luck or a fortunate quirk of fate will change the course of a man's life, a family's fortunes, or even the destiny of a nation. And sometimes luck will repeat itself and from accident or coincidence or mere chance – call it what you like - actions and events will flow that never could have been foreseen. So it was with Bern. Perhaps the small boat that had carried Ragnar across the sea to England was the luckiest little craft that any boat builder had ever fashioned. Now the direction was north and east toward Denmark, the homeland of Bern's victim. Bern was lucky. The weather was fair, the wind was steady, and the tides and currents favoured him with a quick passage across the waters of the North Sea.

Ragnar had many sons and when they heard the tale that Bern told of their father's death they were filled with fury. Bern told them that Ragnar had survived his ordeal in an open boat and that he had been found and taken to Edmund's court at Reedham. There the helpless Viking king had been callously murdered at the young king's command.

The sons of Ragnar swore by their Viking gods that they would be avenged. Thousands of warriors answered the call to arms and a mighty fleet of ships was gathered to carry them swiftly across the sea to East Anglia. The heathen army burned its way across the land. The smoke of burning towns and villages, monasteries and churches, rich men's halls and poor men's cottages, filled the sky. Edmund gathered together what forces he could but they were no match for the invaders.

In the words of the Anglo-Saxon Chronicle, 'The heathen army went into winter quarters at Thetford. That same winter King Edmund fought them, but the Danes won, and they killed the king and conquered the kingdom of East Anglia.' Edmund was forced to go on the run and there is a legend that he was betrayed to the invaders by a wedding party as he hid under a bridge. Ragnar's son Ivar the Boneless [so called because he was a remarkable contortionist] offered Edmund his life if he would renounce his Christian religion and accept Ivar as his king. When Edmund refused his fate was sealed.

He was tied to a tree and the Danish archers used him as a target until Edmund's body bristled with as many arrows as a hedgehog does with spines. Then his head was chopped off. It was November 20, 869. When the Danes moved on some of Edmund's trusted companions came in search of their king's body. They soon found the headless corpse but they could find no sign of the head. Then, as they searched in the thickets of thorns and brambles they heard the king's voice calling 'Here. Here. Here'. To their amazement they found that the call came from the lips of Edmund's severed head which lay between the paws of a guardian grey wolf. When they placed Edmund's head and body together the two parts were miraculously reunited. The site of Edmund's martyrdom is disputed among historians but tradition associates it most closely with the picturesque Suffolk village of Hoxne in the Waveney valley.

So began the cult of St Edmund. During later Danish invasions his body was moved from place to place until eventually it ended up in a shrine in the rich and powerful monastery in the Suffolk town that bears his name, Bury St Edmunds. Such was Edmund's subsequent fame and status that he was regarded as England's patron saint until replaced by St George whose dragon-slaying exploits were more to the taste of medieval English warrior knights.

So who was the king of England who was killed by a ghost? And who was that ghost? The king who died by the hand of a ghost was Sweyn Forkbeard, King of Denmark, and for a few months, the king of England too. And as we tell his story you will notice some more coincidences and some more instances of history apparently repeating itself.

Sweyn was another of those Danish warrior-kings whose violent activities made the life of ordinary people grim and miserable. He fought battles across England, even besieging London until he was bought off with Danegeld by King Ethelred the Unready. Then he made himself king of Norway before turning his attentions to England again. When Ethelred ordered the massacre of all the Danes in England, one of those killed was Sweyn's sister. Back came Sweyn with an army to burn Norwich and Thetford and spread death and destruction across the land. Time and again Sweyn returned with his army during the closing years of Ethelred's unhappy reign and time and again the English paid him to go away. Then, in the autumn of 1013, Ethelred fled abroad and Sweyn was recognised as king of England by right of conquest but his triumph did not last long.

In the early weeks of 1014 he was up to his usual gangster game of demanding money with menaces. From his hall in Gainsborough he issued another demand. This time he declared that he would sack the town of Bury St Edmunds along with its shrine and monastery unless yet more protection money was handed over. This was the cue for St Edmund to put an end to Sweyn's rapacious regime. On February 3, 1014, the violent and hairy pirate king met his end at the hands of the ghost of England's patron saint.

The Ghost that Killed a King

At least that is the story that was recorded in some of the old chronicles. This is how some of the monks recorded the tale. They said Sweyn was a naturally cruel man and he and his army spread rape and slaughter across the land. Their crimes were too numerous to count. Then he dared to demand money from Bury St Edmunds, 'the town where the uncorrupted body of the precious martyr Edmund rested.' If the tribute was not paid Sweyn said he would burn the town and its abbey to the ground, slaughter all the townsfolk and torture the monks to death in a variety of hideous ways. It was something no one had ever dared to do before. And then he made things even worse by having the audacity to mock and scorn the saint's character and reputation.

This was all too much and as he was repeating his threats while surrounded by his army 'divine vengeance put a stop to his blasphemy'. Only Sweyn could see the ghost of St Edmund coming towards him. 'Help!' he cried. 'Look, St Edmund is coming to kill me.' As he was speaking the saint ran him through with a spear and he fell from the stallion he was mounted on and suffered great agony until twilight when he died most miserably.

Of course, this tale of an avenging ghost is dismissed as fiction and monkish propaganda by modern historians. They say that Sweyn, who was in his early fifties when he died, was not killed by a spook with a spear but his demise was probably the result of the injuries he suffered when he fell off his horse. A couple of other little known facts about Sweyn that might be useful in a pub quiz one day – his reign was the second shortest by a king of England, and he was never actually crowned king of England.

And there is another little twist in the tale. Two years after the death of Sweyn his son Cnut became the undisputed king of England, again by right of conquest. His attitude to the cult of St Edmund was very different to that of his father. He honoured Edmund even to the point of adding to the saint's link with Broadland.

On the north bank of the River Bure not far from Ludham are the scanty but distinctive remains of the abbey of St Benet at Holm of which more will be told later. The abbey had been established way back around 800 AD at a time when the small English kingdoms like Wessex, Mercia and Northumbria were fighting each other for supremacy. Then came the Viking invasions and St Benet's was one of the monasteries torched by the vengeful sons of Ragnar in their campaign against Edmund.

Then around about the time that Sweyn and his army were causing murder and mayhem up and down the land a handful of monks reoccupied the island site [hence the name Holm which means small island] and dedicated themselves and their very rough and ready church to St Benedict. In medieval England 'Benedict' was often abbreviated to 'Benet' so that's why it's called St Benet at Holm.

When the astute and politically canny Cnut became king he showed the small fraternity his favour and he also decided to help foster the growing importance of the cult of St Edmund. The saint's shrine at Bury was handed over to the care of monks, some of them from St Benet's. Cnut granted them special privileges and he even helped to finance the building of a new church to house the saint's reportedly uncorrupted remains. One story claims that years after his death a pious widow would trim the saint's nails and cut his hair.

There is another tale of St Edmund's ghost putting in an appearance. It happened around the time of the Black Death when the fame of the saint's cult and the wealth of the abbey were causing other clerics to cast envious eyes at them. One of the covetous ones, so the story goes, was the bishop of Norwich who claimed jurisdiction over the abbey. Soon he and the monks were involved in a long and expensive legal dispute until the night when the monk who was on duty at the shrine fell asleep and had a dream.

He saw the long-dead saint rise up from his tomb. Then he saw the abbey's mighty doors open and close as the ghost of Edmund, armed with a shining sword and with a golden crown upon his head, marched off in search of the bishop who was threatening the future of his abbey. Then the sleeping monk saw in his dream the ghost silently return to the shrine room but with the blade of his sword stained with blood. The ghost of Edmund then climbed back into his tomb while another spirit cleaned the sword and returned it to its place among the relics of the saint. When the monk awoke he discovered that the interfering bishop had died unexpectedly and the last words to cross his lips had been, 'St Edmund! St Edmund!'

Even now, many hundreds of years later, there are plenty of links in Broadland with the troubled times of St Edmund and the Danish invasions. There are plenty of place names indicating Danish settlement and the popularity of the cult of St Edmund is reflected in the number of medieval churches that were dedicated to him.

One of those churches dedicated to Edmund is the small thatched and round towered church at Fritton on the Suffolk side of the River Waveney. Inside are very old cartoon-like wall paintings showing the martyrdom of the young king. There is a medieval painted picture of him in the church at Barton Turf along with St Apollonia, the patron of sufferers of toothache. He is also shown holding an arrow on the screen at Stalham church along with two other English saints who were very popular in medieval times, St Edward the Confessor and

St Thomas of Canterbury.

Also at Stalham you can find a very old picture of the less famous hermit saint, St Roch. He became the patron of plague sufferers after it was said that he had survived a bout of the pestilence thanks to the attentions of a dog that brought him food in the depths of the woods where he lived. Roch is shown with a plague sore on his thigh revealed by his rolled down hose. Another Broadland church with a medieval picture of Edmund is at Ludham. In the floor of the nave is a memorial to a remarkable medical man whose ministrations we might assume were more successful than calling down the aid of Roch for the plague or Apollonia for toothache. He was Richard Cooke who died in his seventies in 1753. According to the eulogy carved on the stone he was a man peculiarly fitted for his profession as a surgeon and thanks to his 'unwearied diligence and long experience' he was equal to almost anything he undertook. That must have been a great comfort to his patients.

The Demon Dog of the Vikings

While it is very unlikely that you'll come across the ghost of St Edmund in Reedham or anywhere else in Broadland, there is a manifestation that you might encounter just about anywhere in the area, and in many other places in Norfolk and Suffolk too.

I have used the word 'manifestation' to make the point that he is definitely not so much the spectre of a dead person, but more of a permanently Earth-bound phantom. His name is Black Shuck and lots of people will tell you that he has links with the days of the Vikings. Others will say that's a load of nonsense and that he was an invention of smugglers. Others say he is nothing more than the product of the Victorians' love of spooky fireside stories that drew on old myths and legends. But the fact is that there are a couple of monsters in Viking mythology that might have been the inspiration for the tales of Black Shuck. There was Garm, the monster dog that guarded the land of the dead, and Fenrir, the ferocious wolf that is destined to break free from his chain and devour Odin at Ragnarok – the final battle of the gods. In Norse mythology Odin is avenged by his son Vidar who kills the beasts by stabbing his sword between the beasts' gaping jaws.

My bet is that Shuck is an English version of Garm because the scariest thing that is said about him is that if you see him you'll be dead within a year. I'll tell you a tale that seems to support that claim a little later.

Shuck's usual beat is along the coast of Norfolk and Suffolk with occasional ventures inland to the lonely country lanes of the villages within Broadland and the Suffolk sandlings. There is no consensus about his appearance and character – some people have reported him as a big black dog with just one fiery red eye set in the middle of his head like Cyclops. Others have said that he has two eyes as big as plates that glow like red-hot burning coals.

Lots of people have told me tales about Black Shuck. It's very likely that many of these stories are second, third or even fourth-hand. I suspect that many of them are – and dare I say it? – the reworked and much embellished versions of tales that they have read in books and magazines. Certainly in recent years more words have been printed in newspapers, books and magazines about East Anglia's phantom dog than ever before. But I have been told one or two tales about the black beast that appear to be remarkably original, and, as far as I am aware, have not been recorded elsewhere.

Shaggy Black Shuck – and he's usually described as having a very shaggy and unkempt coat - seems to go back a long way into history, perhaps even to the times of Ragnar Lothbrog [shaggy breeches] and St Edmund. Some people say Shuck gets his name from the old Saxon scucca or sceocca meaning demon or devil. The trouble is that there don't seem to be any written references naming Old Shuck before the 19th century. Yes, there are the well-documented tragic events of August 4, 1577, that occurred at Bungay beside the River Waveney which some people claim were caused by Shuck.

But just as poor old Oliver Cromwell and his Ironsides get the blame for lots of things they didn't do, so it is pretty clear that shaggy Old Shuck was innocent of the death and destruction that happened on that August day. Briefly what happened was this. An extraordinary 'great and powerful tempest' blew up and it resulted in lightning strikes on two churches, one at Bungay and one a few miles away at Blythburgh. The storm burst overhead just when the churches were packed with their Sunday morning congregations. Both buildings were damaged and some people were killed. At

The Demon Dog of the Vikings

Bungay the storm was so frightening that those in the church were struck with 'such a sore and sudden fear that they were in a manner robbed of their right wits.' They thought Doomsday had come.Two men had their necks wrung and another was left 'shrunk up' like a piece of leather scorched by a fire.

Those who witnessed the events declared that 'the horrible shaped thing' that flew in through the doors was the Devil in the form of a fiery black dog. It's no real surprise that the survivors blamed the Devil rather than thunderbolts or whirlwinds because the 1570s were a time when the English witch-hunting craze was beginning to gather momentum. How times change! Now you can see a shaggy black dog in Bungay every day – his image is used as a weather vane in the market place and he's even on the town's coat of arms.

But tales of Shuck don't usually tell of him savagely killing people or attacking them when they congregate in large numbers. There may be different opinions about what he looks like – having two huge fiery eyes or just one, and being as big as a calf, and sometimes even being headless – but one thing that most people say about him is that he's usually seen in lonely out-of-the-way places like deserted beaches, silent riverbanks, narrow country lanes, or close to dark and forbidding graveyards at night. In fact, almost anywhere as long as it's far from the madding crowd!

Many who claim to have encountered Shuck say his howl is far more scary and haunting than his wild appearance. It is often claimed that he is most likely to appear on a stormy winter night when a gale is howling and the waves of the North Sea are hurling themselves against the vulnerable land. Then, if you venture out, you might hear Shuck's frightening howls rising above the din and tumult of the restless elements. Those who have heard him howling say that it is enough to make your blood run cold and send icy shivers racing up and down the spine.

But the most frightening component of the whole Shuck legend is that if you are unlucky enough to meet him face to face it is a portent of death. His appearance means you will be dead before another full year has passed. It's a claim that would be easy to verify if there was records of the people who claim to have met him and when they died. But as that's unlikely to happen all I can do is tell you a tale that was told to me many years ago in a pub in Cheshire by someone who had moved away from Norfolk after having spent their childhood near the coast. The area between Winterton and Happisburgh was not exactly overflowing with a variety of employment options for a go-ahead young man in the years after the Second World War. It was a tale he had from his grandfather. Here are his words.

'He was a bit of a strange old cove was Mr Jerome Albert Cloudy. I think that's what his name was. I'm not totally sure of the Jerome and the Albert but the Cloudy was right. It's an unusual name right enough but you'll find people of that name in the telephone directory. Anyway grandfather called him Mr Jack on account of his initials. Somehow grandfather had landed himself with the job of arranging the accommodation for Mr Jack when he wanted to come up to Norfolk for his holiday. He'd come every year for ten days at the end of September and early October. He was a strange old cove but he was regular in his habits.

'First off grandfather arranged for him to stay at a hotel but Mr Cloudy didn't like that so from then on he'd usually rent a house though on one occasion he did stay at the vicarage. Anyway, as I said, Mr Jack was a strange old cove. He liked being by himself when he was here. I'm not sure where he came from, London I think but I could be wrong. He never used to talk about where he was from or what he did. One thing was for sure, he weren't short of money, so I reckon he must have had a pretty good job somewhere.

'Anyway, he'd send a postcard every February regular as clockwork saying he'd be coming in September as usual and saying he'd want accommodation near such-and-such a place. I know, you're thinking we could tell where he came from by the picture and postmark on the postcard. Well, we couldn't because they were always postcards with foreign scenes on them like Paris or Rome or Brussels.

'Anyway, the accommodation. Grandfather would see to it and then four or five days before Mr Jack were due he'd get a telegram giving the time of the train he intended to be on and which station he was to be collected from – Hemsby, Martham, Stalham. Lots of little places had stations in those days. Grandfather would go and meet him with a trap but sometimes Mr Jack would arrive with the carrier. One time he got things wrong and turned up at Martham with the Wednesday carrier from Yarmouth. They say he never uttered a word the whole journey long.

'Reckon it were silence and solitude what he wanted so that's what he got. He'd have his breakfast at seven o'clock on the dot, then at eight-thirty he'd set off with some cheese sandwiches and a bottle of ginger beer stuffed in a satchel and off he'd go, striding down the road. He was a right odd sight because he'd turn his head from side to side as though he was sniffing the air. Then he'd look down at the ground and a moment later he'd be looking up at the sky. Off he'd go and he wouldn't come back till evening. I told you he were a strange old cove.

'One year he arrived with a bike in the goods van. The roads weren't like they are now. Lots of pot holes and ruts on the country lanes then. Trouble was Mr Jack weren't no good on a bike. He'd go swerving all over the road. Didn't have no proper sense of balance, see. He fell off a fair few times and ended up with cuts and bruises and his jacket and trousers got torn. After two or three days he gave the bike to grandfather and went back to walking. That made life a lot safer for him and for everybody else.

'Anyway, it were the year grandfather moved into a new house that Mr Jack started to change his ways. It were quite a big old place, not more than a mile from the beach. Grandfather were right busy that year so he decided to put Mr Jack up in the new house and he set a couple of rooms aside for him. Mr Jack didn't say nothing so grandfather reckoned it were all right with him. Anyway, off he'd go on his walks same as ever.

'Then, one day - and a right glorious day it had been too – the evening was coming on and there was that still and heavy feeling about it. It started clouding over and you just knew that the weather was building up for one of them real good thunderstorms. But Mr Jack was nowhere to be seen. Grandfather kept popping out and looking down the road, but there was no sign of him. First off the rain wasn't too bad. Still no sign of him. Then it broke. Thunder and lightning and rare old torrential rain. If I said it came down like stair rods a lot of young folks wouldn't know what I mean. Don't see many stair rods these days, do you!

'Anyway, it certainly did come down like stair rods. A right old storm it was. The sky went as black as your hat and you could hear the thunder roaring and rolling like cannons. And then striding up the road came Mr Jack. Well, he wasn't so much striding as sort of staggering and tottering at the same time. He was in a right state. He was like a drowned rat. He'd lost his hat and was soaked to the skin. Grandfather dashed out with a brolly but the wind was so strong that it was almost blown out of his hands and in a couple of ticks he was soaked through as well. When they came through the front door they were dripping water everywhere and that didn't please grandmother none, particularly as she'd had a new bit of carpet put down in the hall and up the stairs.

'She shoved the two of them through to the scullery, threw a couple of towels and some dry clothes in after them and shut the door on them. When things had calmed down and they were in their dry clothes Mr Jack did something he'd never done before. He asked grandfather if he could eat his evening meal with them. Grandfather was a bit befuzzled by that but grandmother said she had nothing against it so that evening the three of them sat round the table in the kitchen. Grandmother said they weren't going to eat in the front room after such a to-do as had happened, not even for Mr Jack.

'Grandfather said that it was turning out to be just about the quietest meal he'd ever had when all unexpected like Mr Jack started talking. First he made a joke about him and grandfather getting soaked to the skin. But it was a pretty feeble sort of a joke. Then he went on about the storm, saying it was a rare one. Grandfather and grandmother didn't know what to make of it so they just let him rattle on. Suddenly there was a real loud crack of thunder overhead and they all sort of ducked. That was when Mr Jack came out with it. He said that as he was hurrying back up the lane, all drenched and cold, he thought he'd heard a right frightening howling noise not far behind him. It was the sort of howling that had made the hair stand up on the back of his neck. He said he'd never heard the like of it before. Grandfather looked at grandmother, and she looked at him and she gave him a little nod like.

'Grandfather sort of nudged his empty plate a bit away from him, turned to Mr Jack and said,'Oh, so you heard Old

Shuck, did you? Can't say as I did. Not this time. Not that I'd want to and that's for sure.'

At this point my informant broke off from his story telling. For a few moments he was silent and then he pushed his empty glass across the table as a sign that it was to be recharged. As I rose to obey he looked me full in the eyes and, in a slow and deliberate monotone, he repeated the last few phrases that he had attributed to his grandfather. ..... 'So you heard Old Shuck, did you? Can't say as I did. Not this time. Not that I'd want to and that's for sure.'

With our glasses full again he continued.

'Mr Jack finished the food on his plate, wiped his fingers and the corners of his mouth with his napkin – he always insisted on having a napkin – and then gave both grandfather and grandmother a bit of an odd sort of stare. 'What did you say I heard?' he said in a tone that was close to being a demand.

'Grandmother was first to react. She stood up and began to gather up the plates. 'Don't go on so with your old tales,' she said to grandfather. Mr Jack waved a hand. 'Old tales! Please, tell me your old tales. I wish to hear them. I am most interested.'

'At that moment there was an insistent banging at the front door. Grandmother hurried away to see who it was and a few moments later two men in rain-smeared oilskins with dripping sou'westers in their hands were standing in the kitchen close behind Mr Jack. Grandmother returned hard on their heels. 'Out! Out! Both of you. Out you go! Out! Out the back way!' she said sternly. One of the men began to mutter an apology.

'Hold you on a minute, mother,' said grandfather rising from his chair. There were further hastily muttered greetings and apologies from the two of them before one declared,

'T'ain't no night to be out. Specially not no stranger. '

'The second man cut in. 'We was just makin' certain sure your holiday lodger was inside. Some on us have heard 'him' so we just wanted to make sure your lodger-fellow was indoors behind four walls and not wandering round out there.'

'As if to emphasise his concern the room was suddenly lit by a distant curtain of sheet lightning quickly followed by another boom of thunder overhead.

'We were passing so we.... reckon we'd best be going,' said the first man. 'Reckon you had,' declared grandmother sternly. 'And out the backway you go, both of you.' They departed through the back door leaving two puddles of rainwater on the lino which were quickly wiped away by grandmother. That done she turned to the two men seated at the kitchen table and announced that pudding was ready for them as wanted some.

'The next day was bright and sunny. Just perfect for going for a walk. But Mr Jack he didn't go nowhere. He had his breakfast same as always and grandmother packed his satchel with sandwiches and a bottle of ginger beer same as always. But he stayed put and he started pestering grandfather and grandmother with loads of questions about the happenings of the previous night.

'What was that howling noise he'd heard? Who or what was Old Shuck? Was it a man or a beast? Why had two strangers in oilskins been so concerned about his whereabouts? He wanted answers and he declared that he was staying put till he got some.

'Eventually to keep him quiet grandfather and grandmother sat down with him in the garden and told him all the old tales they knew about Old Shuck. They told him where he was said to roam and how his howling was mostly heard when a storm was brewing. And they told him that to come face to face with was a certain sign of death with a twelvemonth.

'At the end of it Mr Jack said not a word for quite a spell. Then he gave grandfather and grandmother one of his strange stares and asked them if, hands on hearts, they believed any of the old tales about Shuck such as they'd just told him.

'Grandmother fidgeted some in her chair then grandfather he looked Mr Jack square in the eye and said, 'Maybe I do and maybe I don't. Come on, mother, we got us some work to do.'

'From that moment on things were different. Mr Jack became all quiet again. He hardly spoke another word. He started going off again by himself again and mostly it was to the beach where he'd just walk and walk. Sometimes he'd stand on the sea bank just staring and staring. People would report seeing him standing and staring for hours. 'We knew he was a strange old cove,' they'd say to grandfather, 'but now he's stranger than ever.' And when he was gone there was a lot of talk about him asking folk to tell him all they knew about Old Shuck.

'Grandfather and grandmother were pleased to see the back of him at the end of his holiday that year. But not six weeks had passed before there was a postcard from him saying he'd be coming to stay again in a week's time. And so he did. Grandfather could have told him to get back on the train but he needed the money what with the move to the bigger house.

'He spent his time same as before. He'd be seen just standing and staring. Even the November weather didn't seem to bother him none. Then back he went to where he came from but, blow me, a postcard arrived not long after Christmas and a few days later he was back again. The same again in March. He came for a week in April and then he stayed most of May. Grandmother was getting real concerned about what was going on. It wasn't just that most of the work fell on her but she reckoned Mr Jack had brought a gun along with him the last couple of times, but grandfather wouldn't hear of it.

'Mr Jack came as usual in September. But this time he came earlier in the month and stayed for four weeks. He took all his meals alone in his room and scarcely uttered a word. If he wanted anything he'd scribble it down on a piece of paper and leave it at the top of the stairs. Not only was his behaviour getting stranger, his appearance was changing too. He'd never been what you'd call a picture of health, but he'd seemed 'sound enough in wind and whistle' as grandfather used to say. But during the summer he'd started going real scrawny. When he left he was more of a scarecrow than a man.

'Ten days later a postcard arrived. On the front was a picture of a statue by some Italian fellow by the name of Bernini. It was of a hairy Roman god carrying off a woman and in the bottom corner was this three-headed dog. The only words on it other than grandfather's name and address were 'Old Shuck, I heard him in that storm. I saw him too. Mr Jack.' Around those words was a thick black border like they used to do on those old fashioned 'in memoriam' cards that people used to have printed.

'Needless to say that was the last postcard grandfather ever had from Mr Jack.'

It's all too easy nowadays for people to ridicule the old tales and giggle at the idea a of phantom dog that foretells someone's death. But consider this – reports regularly appear of large wild cat-like or dog-like beasts being seen in various places around the country. Can we be one hundred per cent certain that they are all escaped big cats living wild or nothing more than the figments of witnesses' imaginations?

I'm pleased to report that the idea that Old Shuck or Black Shuck, call him what you will, is a terrifying and infallible portent of death does not occur everywhere. I have also heard it told that in some places he is seen as a gentle guardian who keeps an eye on travellers at night and sees them safely home. That was the tale I was told more than once when I lived on the Norfolk and Suffolk border not far from the coast. So take your pick – Old Shuck is a portent of death; the folk memory of Viking days long ago; a demon dog that spreads fire and destruction; an invention of smugglers eager to keep people away from beaches; or a guardian of travellers out alone on dark nights.

Whether he exists or not it seems that shaggy Old Shuck was the inspiration for one of the classics of English detective literature. The claim is that back in 1901 Sir Arthur Conan Doyle, the creator of the super sleuth Sherlock Holmes, spent a few days on holiday on the Norfolk coast. While he was there he heard the tale of Black Shuck and a year later 'The Hound of the Baskervilles' was published. But the mystery of the fearsome black dog with a blood-chilling howl was set in the wilds of Dartmoor and not along the lonely beaches of Norfolk and Suffolk.

If you are prepared to stay up till after midnight on a certain night in April you too can witness a macabre event that will tell you who among your friends and neighbours is marked for death in the coming year. At least that is what is said to happen around midnight on St Mark's Eve, April 24.

As one Victorian poet put it –
The ghosts of all whom Death shall doom
Within the coming year
In pale procession walk the gloom,
Amid the silence drear.

It was a widespread superstition and one that the Church

frowned on. The belief was that if you sat in the church porch during the hour before and the hour after midnight on April 24 you would see the spectres of those who were going to die or suffer serious illness in the year ahead. They would march up the path and into the church. Those that remained inside would die, those that came out again would fight off their illness. It was not a vigil likely to be kept by the fainthearted in the nights before street lights, late night entertainment and almost constant traffic.

One chap who was happy to do it many years ago was the landlord of the Maids Head, the old coaching inn opposite St Mary's Church in the middle of Stalham. It was reported that he would keep watch on St Mark's Eve and make a note of who was going to die and who were going to get married. The publican reckoned that he had special powers that allowed him to see the spooky goings on. He said the ones who went in singly were marked for death and those who entered the church in pairs were destined to get married. In one case it was reported that the watchers heard the burial service being uttered as the corpse in its winding sheet floated past. That ghastly spectacle was followed by the sound of rattling bones and earth being shovelled into a grave. The publican of Stalham was proud of his powers but when he came in for criticism for his ghoulish habit he said he never told anyone what he saw.

A Phantom Ship and a Skeleton Crew

O nce they were as much a part of everyday life as were the rivers and broads themselves. Now they are the restored and cherished reminders of a much quieter and slower-paced way of life that has disappeared into the history books.

What were they? They were the wherries – the graceful sailing vessels that transported many of necessities of life up and down the rivers of Broadland. They brought in the imported goods from the sea-going ships that docked at Great Yarmouth and Lowestoft, and they carried Norwich's manufactures and the countryside's agricultural produce to the coast.

Distribution and carriage by water was quicker and cheaper by wherry in the first half of the 19th century. Then came the railways and the wherry business went into decline. Around 1900 there were about 70 of them still operating. By 1930 three in four of them had gone. Some were still being built in the early years of the 20th century but they were usually constructed with passengers, pleasure and leisure in mind rather than the toilsome business of trade.

To behold a wherry gliding past today is an amazing and heart-warming sight. But we should remember that many years ago, in their guise as trading vessels, the wherries on the rivers of Norfolk and Suffolk were often the targets for crooks and villains, some of whom did not stop at murder.

In a churchyard in Bungay there is a memorial headstone to a young man by the name of Henry Scarles. It says he 'was valued when alive and respected now dead'. Poor Henry worked for Mr Kerrison, a merchant at Bungay, and he met his death on February 10, 1787, when he was only 23 years old. It was his bad luck to disturb a gang of robbers – William Hawke, Tom Mayhew and Simon Stannard – when they were busy looting a wherry. Poor Henry was knocked into the water and hit on the head with a quant pole.

The three villains tried to escape the area but they were captured halfway across Suffolk by thief-takers employed by local traders who were fed up with the pilfering and theft that went on. The three were imprisoned in Norwich Castle and at their trial Stannard gave evidence against his two accomplices. Mayhew and Hawke were declared guilty and hanged barely two months after the murder. Justice was often grim and swift in those days. Indeed, through the years of the 19th century there were many instances of cargoes being rifled or even being stolen completely. Some of the villains ended up on the other side of the world in Australia after being sentenced to transportation.

Many of the churchyards of Broadland and along the Norfolk and Suffolk coast have memorials to children and adults, civilians and members of the military, who have lost their lives in drowning accidents on the rivers and broads as well as in the sea. There is one at Barton Turf that tells of the deaths of four brothers who drowned in Barton Broad on Boxing Day 1781. In 1801 a battleship of Nelson's navy, HMS Invincible, was lost as she sailed to join the fleet off Copenhagen. Many of the 400 men who died were buried in Happisburgh churchyard.

In the churchyard at Thurlton there is a headstone carved with a wherry to a man named Joseph Bexfield. He was drowned in August 1809. His demise is recounted in many books about uncanny happenings. It is usually claimed that his death was the result of an unwary man being lured to his death by mysterious lights on the marshes. According to his memorial stone he was 38 and he left 'a disconsolate widow and two children to deplore his loss.' A more mundane explanation that I have been told is that he was sleeping on deck to keep cool on a hot August night. For some reason he fell into the river and drowned. No doubt the truth is in the archives somewhere.

With the wherry being such an important part of the heritage of the Broads, it should come as no surprise to hear that there is a tale of a phantom wherry. It's a tale I have heard many times with a variety of characters in the cast and a variety of places being given for its setting. The wherry is usually called Mayfly but so far I have not seen any evidence that there ever was a wherry of that name.

So here's the story. It is set back in the days when England was changing fast. There was a young queen called Victoria on the throne and she was not many years into her reign. It was also a time when transporting large sums of cash from one place to another could still be a hazardous business.

There was a wealthy merchant who lived and traded in Beccles, that pleasant little market town most of which lies on the Suffolk side of the River Waveney. For reasons best known to himself, the Beccles merchant put a ruffian who went by the nickname of Blood in charge of the wherry Mayfly. Blood was a lucky man indeed because the Mayfly was considered a lucky craft by all who had sailed on her. The appointment was something of a surprise to all the watermen who plied their trade on the rivers and broads of Norfolk and Suffolk because Blood had a most unsavoury reputation. Yes, he was an experienced sailor sure enough, but he was also a violent man with a short temper, a fact to which the scars on his face and his fists gave ample testimony. His rank was resented by many of the other men in the merchant's employ who each considered that they should have won the promotion ahead of such a ruffian.

A Phantom Ship and a Skeleton Crew

One day in June Blood was called into the company office and told that he was to transport a strongbox down the river to Great Yarmouth where it was to be delivered to the safety of a bank. It was a large sum indeed, around half a million pounds. Whether anyone in Beccles has ever had half a million in cash so close at hand, then or now, must be open to debate. Anyway, in an effort to fool any villains who might have got wind of the plan, the merchant's young and beautiful daughter Millie volunteered to go along with the cover story that the chest contained nothing more than a few items from her wardrobe.

In a further effort to hoodwink any conspiracy, an identical box was loaded on a wagon and despatched to Great Yarmouth by road. The problem was that there was a conspiracy to rob and it was fast taking shape in the head of the unscrupulous Captain Blood.

There were few wherries as swift and handy as the Mayfly. Indeed, she could outpace almost any craft on the Waveney, the Yare or the Bure. But on that June morning it seemed that her speed would be of no consequence. The Beccles merchant and the crew began to think she was going nowhere. One thing followed another in a series of minor and irritating mishaps which conspired to postpone her departure. The time lost stretched to two and then three hours, and the affluent Beccles merchant began to fidget and fret at the delay. Then, two hours or more after noon, as though by magic, all the petty accidents ceased.

Blood had his usual crew with him that day – two men, a boy and a dog. The eldest of the three was a sour-tempered and furtive man called George Grubb aged somewhere around the forty-year mark. He, like Blood, was an impatient and brooding man, and he considered himself to be the second in command, though no such rank existed. His head was square and his neck and arms and body had been made thick and strong by years of heaving heavy cargo. The second man was much younger. His name was Nick. His face was open and honest, and in his eyes there was the scarcely concealed light of a great affection for the merchant's pretty daughter. The fetch-and-carry boy Davey was barely across the threshold of working life, and already his body carried plenty of bruises administered by the fists and boots of both Blood and the man who supposed himself to be second in command. The dog kept clear of everyone except Nick and the boy.

'Don't you worry about the lateness of the hour,' said Blood to the sweating and fretting merchant. 'The Mayfly will make up the time. Your money will be stowed safe and sound in that Yarmouth bank vault long afore you taste your supper.'

The summer breeze was strong and steady from the southwest. Unhindered, it picked up some pace across the Gillingham marshes. At Blood's command the big black sail was raised and soon they were gliding away from the wharf. Almost silently they followed the twists and turns of the Waveney with their little dinghy bobbing and bouncing along in their wake. They passed the staithe at Burgh St Peter and then their course changed from easterly to northerly. Without a hint of any further mishap they glided on down river between Wheatacre and Somerleyton Marshes, and on passed St Olaves with its old riverside inn and the even older crumbling and ivy-clad remains of its priory.

The June afternoon was cooling fast as they came up on the walls of the Roman fort at Burgh Castle to starboard. 'Grubb,' bellowed Blood, 'you hold her steady and you Miss Millie get yourself below. And you go with her boy.' Millie did not like his tone of voice but she made no complaint when she saw the hard look in his eyes that declared he would brook neither argument nor challenge.

Nick witnessed everything from his station on the bow and he detected a feeling of unease and suspicion growing in his mind. The more he thought of what had happened that day the more he did not like what he had heard and seen. He watched Blood move close to Grubb and grip tight the steersman's right shoulder while his mouth whispered words into his left ear. Nick could not hear what words were spoken. Grubb seemed about to voice a complaint or perhaps an objection but the captain's grip tightened. A grimace of pain flashed across Grubb's mouth before he nodded in compliance. Blood nodded too and laughed and thumped him twice across the back with a force that shook the steersman from his head to his knees.

Blood took back control of the Mayfly and ordered the sail to be lowered. And when the Mayfly was moored close to the walls of the ancient fortress Nick's suspicion deepened, but he held his tongue. Young Davey brought them food and drink but there was little conversation. They watched each other in silence as the sky began to dim and darkness advanced across the world. Another hour passed and Blood got to his feet and stared hard at the western sky. 'It's time,' he yelled. Suddenly all was activity. The sail was raised. Mooring lines were taken aboard. Blood shouted more commands and the Mayfly searched for the gentle but ever weakening breeze of the early night.

Like the others, Nick felt the wherry gather pace as they entered Breydon Water. It was what Blood had been waiting for. The tide was ebbing fast and it had the Mayfly in its quickening grasp. It was a time of real peril but Blood knew his business and he knew his ship. 'No lights!' he bellowed when Nick made to hoist a lantern at the bow. 'But...' It was the only word that Nick was allowed to utter before Blood shouted his command again. 'No lights!'

Nick retreated from the bow and he could see Grubb standing close at Blood's left shoulder. There was cold contempt and thin-lipped hostility upon his face. The boy had slipped away below with the dog. The silence was broken by Millie emerging from the cabin in agitated haste. There was apprehension and deep anxiety in her usually soft and youthful voice. 'What's going on?' she cried. 'We should have been in Yarmouth hours ago. My father will not....'

A blow across the mouth turned her words into sobs and cries of pain and distress. She wiped a hand across her shivering lips and stared in disbelief at the blood that dripped from her fingers. 'Get below, now, and stay there!' shouted Blood, raising his fist again. Millie turned to obey.

The cruelty was too much for Nick. He too raised a hand. But before he could utter either a syllable or sound Blood had one hand upon his throat, its fingers stabbing into his flesh like the talons of a giant claw. In the same instant the captain's other hand was transformed into a bludgeoning fist that smashed into Nick's face with the force of a fourteen pound hammer. The first blow broke his nose. The second blow rendered the young man's resistance as short lived and futile as were his final sharp and rapid gasps for breath. The fist smashed again into Nick's face. Then again. And then a dozen times the rings on Blood's fingers cut and ripped and tore the young man's face into a bloody ball of bone and flesh and sightless eyes. Nick was as dead as butchers' meat when his body hit the water.

Blood turned and stared at Grubb. 'Nothing, captain, nothing,' squeaked the would-be mate. The retreating tide hastened the Mayfly across the fast-emptying expanse of Breydon Water. Expertly Blood held her where the flow was fastest and deepest. In silence they made the turn and began the three-mile run south toward the sea past the wharves of Yarmouth harbour.

No challenge came from the shore. The only sound that came to their ears was that of straining ropes and timbers. The night became colder and Blood began to taste the tang of salt upon his lips. It was a taste he knew well. It was a taste he'd tasted across seven seas. His ears detected a new sound. It was the sound of sand and stones being swept and scoured and sieved by a restless sea. He smiled. He'd made it. All that lay in front of him now were the world's wide oceans and a star-littered sky.

'Grubb, you take her now,' growled Blood. 'I've got me some business below with that pretty young thing. And Master Grubb, don't you go doing anything unwise. I don't like doing unwise things. You doing something unwise would vex me, Mister Grubb, and I get awful angry when I get vexed. So no suprises, Mr Grubb.' Blood gave emphasis to his words by moving one hand onto the ivory handle of the long bladed knife at his belt.

Grubb said nothing. Half a minute later he heard Blood's deep-throated shouts answered by Millie's screams. The sounds of the violent struggle did not last long. It was replaced by an awful silence that was broken in turn by angry masculine growls and the helpless sobbings of a young woman which soon escalated into shrieks and shouts. Footsteps. Millie emerged onto the deck with blood seeping from her mouth and lips, and those few clothes that she hugged about her body were torn and stained.

Blood came close behind, a bottle held in one hand. His free hand grabbed Millie and threw her back into the cabin. 'Stay in there. And get this into your pretty head – the Mayfly's mine; that there strong box is mine; and you're mine too! Body and soul!'

Blood studied the stars and pulled on the bottle while the Mayfly was swept on by the chill sea breeze.

'Cap'n, a word if you please' said Grubb, his piping voice as low and obsequious as was his demeanour. 'If you'd be good enough to allow it, cap'n, I'll take my share - and that a small share to be sure – from the strong box below. I can take the dinghy and if I strike the beach near Benacre or Covehithe while it's still dark I could be long gone on the road to London before either you or me see the first streak of dawn.'

'So that's your plan is it, Grubb?' replied the skipper, his tone as cold as an east wind in January.

'I'll not say a word. You have my solemn word on that, cap'n.'

'Your everlasting silence, eh? Your solemn word, eh? Well, Mr Grubb, that's comforting to know.'

Grubb nodded and for a few seconds the moonlight caught his thin ingratiating grin, a grin that revealed the foul tobacco-blackened stumps of his teeth and the cowardly curl of his mouth.

'My solemn word, cap'n,' he muttered again.

'Your everlasting silence,' whispered Blood.

'Everlasting, yes, cap'n. You can depend on it,' murmured Grubb.

Grubb was as good as his word. Those few muted, almost inaudible words were the last to pass his lips. Blood grabbed the would-be mate's hair, yanked it back until his throat was stretched and taut. Then, with the precision and confidence of a surgeon dissecting a body for the instruction of a class of medical students, he sliced Grubb's jugular with the razor sharp tip of the blade that he had pulled from his belt.

Yes, Grubb's silence was everlasting.

Blood pulled again on the bottle of spirits. A feeling of warm satisfaction seeped through his bones. The Mayfly has not been built for the open sea but he knew her better than any man alive. He would sail her to America if he had to. Or to India or China. He'd take her anywhere he pleased. And he'd take the merchant's strongbox and pretty daughter too.

Perhaps it was over-confidence born of crimes successfully completed. Perhaps it was the feeling of warmth and well being that grew with every swig of the rum bottle. Perhaps it was the smug contentment that came from knowing that he now had money enough to last a lifetime. Whatever it was, Blood paid the price.

'What do you want?' he growled when he saw Millie approaching with one hand held against the wounds around her mouth and the other gathering the remains of her dress against her shivering white body. 'Get below, girl!'

Millie made no sound. A hand reached out toward Blood. He sidestepped and smacked her hand away. She gave a sharp whine of pain but reached at him again. 'Get away, girl,' he barked, moving aside again and aiming a blow at her head with the bottle.

But he missed his mark. One foot skidded beneath him. His knee bent and his balance was gone. His other foot went sliding away from him too as it stepped into the slippery glaze of blood on the deck. He reached out to halt his fall. Both his action and his curse were in vain. The widening puddle of blood from Grubb's throat was as slippery as ice and down he went.

But as he stumbled and slipped Millie's nimble fingers grasped at the white ivory handle of his knife. Blood detected her action. He saw the hatred in her eyes. He too reached for the knife. He was half a hundredth of a second too late. Her hands were pulling it from his sheath as he grabbed at it. His fingers tightened not against the hilt but around the blade. He yelled as the well-honed edges slice deep into the flesh of his fingers and hands.

With an ear-splitting shriek of vengeance spilling from her lips, Millie pulled back the knife and thrust the bloody blade deep into Blood's belly. He aimed a flailing fist at her. She ducked. He missed. She felt his warm blood splatter across her face. Then, with a strength and stubbornness born of desperation, she gave another shriek and twisted the blade.

Blood screamed in agony as his own knife screwed deeper and deeper into his vitals. With a last despairing lunge his bloodied hands closed around Millie's neck and he pressed and pressed and pressed.

The moon was high when Davey emerged from his hiding place. He cradled the dog in his arms and the dog licked his cheek. Cautiously he crept along the deck. For a few moments he halted and stared in horror at the bodies. The dog uttered a sharp canine growl and Davey resumed his movement. He lowered the dog into the dinghy, and climbed in beside it. He sawed through the rope with the blade of his small pocket knife and the Mayfly sailed away into the night.

He and the dog were found drifting three days later. When he recovered his strength he returned to Beccles cradling the little dog in his arms. He related all that had happened and the merchant adopted him as a son. The years passed and Davey grew into a man. He prospered in trade, but as he did so the merchant's health declined. He spoke few words and made no demands. But each year, in June, they travelled together to the coast. There, for a day or two either side of midsummer, they would scan the far horizon for the first streaks of dawn. They would stare into the strengthening golden light seeking the black sail of the wherry Mayfly. They never saw it in the dawn.

But some say the Mayfly has been seen in phantom form when summer nights are still and silent. They say that when the waters of the broads are as smooth as mirror glass, when they are painted with moonlight, then sometimes a silver-white phantom ship is seen. It has a young woman standing as still and stiff as any statue at the bow, and behind her there is a white-boned skeleton at the helm.

You can follow one of the main old wherry routes of the past by taking the Wherryman's Way. It is a 35-mile long route for walkers between Norwich and Great Yarmouth.

For much of the way it follows the course of the River Yare and skirts the north side of Breydon Water. The route crosses the river at Reedham ferry and there are many points of interest along the way. Access to the path is available from many points along the route.

Places of interest along the way include the isolated Berney Arms drainage mill, Whitlingham Country Park at the approach to Norwich, and the village of Reedham itself. A path that follows the River Chet leads to Loddon with its variety of facilities.

Along the way you will be treading in the footsteps of Billy Bluelight. Billy – his real name was William Cullum - a rather eccentric character who died in 1949.

He made his name by racing the steam pleasure boats that carried passengers on pleasure trips up and down the river Yare. He would jog along attired in a cricket cap, a white shirt bearing an array of home-made medals, and a pair of knee-length shorts held up by an old fashioned belt.

Billy would arrive at the boat stops along the river and greet boat and passengers with his rhyme –

My name is Billy Bluelight, my age is forty-five,

I hope to get to Carrow Bridge before the boat arrive.

Why he called himself Bluelight no one seems to know. Certainly he was a colourful character. So much so that like Queen Victoria, Lord Nelson, Robin Hood and assorted other kings and dukes from history, he had a pub named after him.

A Little Bit of History

How times have changed! Once upon a time East Anglia was the richest and most densely populated region in all England and for several centuries Norwich was second only to London in population and importance.

At the time of the Norman Conquest it had around 6,000 inhabitants and that made it a very big place indeed in England in 1066. Down the centuries Norwich became so populous and wealthy that eventually they said it had a church for every Sunday of the year and a pub for every day of the year. Yes, it's hard to think of Norfolk being one of the richest, most developed and 'industrial' parts of England. But William the Conqueror, one of the biggest land-grabbers in English history, certainly understood it because the Domesday Book lists 241 Norfolk land holdings against his name.

Nowadays Norfolk is perceived by people living beyond its borders as a predominantly rural county, a place to escape to far from the stress and the noise and the pollution of life in the big cities. When asked to describe Norfolk, many people from beyond its borders will give a smile and then quote Noel Coward's quip, 'Very flat, Norfolk' and leave it at that.

But Norfolk is a county of contrasts. Around the coast are wide sandy beaches and picturesque small harbours. There are the heaths and forests of Breckland and the wide open spaces of the Fens. It is a county that has numerous small, picture-postcard villages and attractive market towns. Its capital, Norwich, is a blend of the historic and the modern. In the words of George Borrow, a writer who was popular in the 19th century but is now often neglected, Norwich is a fine city indeed. George travelled widely and spoke many languages so his accolade must carry the authority of experience. But cynics from outside might say that George was a bit partisan in his praise because he was Norfolk born and bred.

He wrote his best and most popular works when he lived at Oulton Broad which is the only broad in Suffolk. And that brings us to Broadland, an area unlike any other. It is truly unique. Indeed, one fact that is often forgotten is that the Broads are man-made. They are the products of a lot of backbreaking toil a long time ago.

Roughly speaking Broadland is that quadrant bounded by two lines drawn north-east and south-east from Norwich and joined by the curve of the coast. Very old maps call the seas off Norfolk 'the limitless north sea' and 'the eastern sea'. Later it became the German Sea. In the northern half of that rough quadrant the rivers Ant and Thurne join the Bure. In the southern half the Waveney joins the Yare at the southern end of Breydon Water. The Chet is a navigable tributary of the Yare. The Waveney forms the boundary between Norfolk and Suffolk for most of its length but it is navigable only as far as Geldeston, a few miles to the west of Beccles. Much of the Waveney is outside this 'broadland' area. Most of the Broads are in the northern and wholly Norfolk half of the segment.

These rivers flow into each other on their way to the sea, eventually finding the sea at Great Yarmouth. That said there is restricted access from the Waveney via Oulton Dyke and Oulton Broad to Lake Lothing and the sea. Some people say the name Lake Lothing and the old Hundred of Lothingland to the north of it preserve the name of that semi-mythical Viking, Ragnar Lothbrog, who drifted across the North Sea in a open boat and ended up at Reedham. Old maps, however, show it as 'Lovingland'.

The Broads are man-made lakes of different shapes and sizes, but it was not until the 1950s that this was understood.

Instead of being the shallow natural lakes people thought they were, they proved to be old peat pits which over time had filled with water. Something of a population explosion occurred in East Anglia in the century after the Norman Conquest and in east Norfolk the demand for wood to use as fuel and building material exhausted the supply. To fill the demand for fuel people turned to using peat and pits were dug near settlements in the river valleys. The village of Barton Turf preserves the memory of those days in its name.

With the changes to the environment came changes to the pattern of life for many of the inhabitants, particularly in the marshland areas. Here cattle were grazed and fattened in summer, reeds were cut for thatching, and eels, fish and wildfowl were caught for the table.

Daniel Defoe, the author of 'Robinson Crusoe', came this way around 1720. He noted how skinny cattle from the cold and barren mountains of Scotland were brought to Norfolk to be fattened for the table. He called them 'runts' and said they would ' feed so eagerly on the rich pasture in these marshes, that they thrive in an unusual manner, and grow monstrously fat; and the beef is so delicious for taste that the inhabitants prefer 'em to the English cattle.' As well as beef, Norfolk provided plenty of geese and turkeys for London's dinner tables, Mr Defoe noting that flocks up to a thousand strong were marched off to the capital around autumn time. A more fastidious 19th century visitor described the marshlands as consisting mainly of 'ooze'.

The upper river valleys are often fringed by woods and farmland and in some places the rivers are edged by the staithes and houses of the villages through which they flow. By contrast marshland offers a very different landscape. It is flat with scarcely a tree or a hedge to be seen. It is criss-crossed by drainage dykes and the most eye-catching structures are often the old drainage wind pumps that once scooped up water from the dykes and drains and tipped it into the rivers.

The 19th century was the age of the wherry and the rivers and broads of east Norfolk and north-east Suffolk served as the heavy transport network supplying the region's commercial and industrial needs. Then the railways came along and took much of the traffic. Then, in the 1880s, Broadland was discovered by holidaymakers.

George Davies, a lawyer by profession, came from Shropshire on the other side of England. He worked in Norwich and immediately developed a great affection for the rivers and broads. He wrote a book called 'The Swan and her Crew' about three young friends who sailed the waterways on a home-made boat. That adventure story for the young was followed by information handbooks describing the waterways in detail. Among the pieces of advice he offered was the suggestion that lusty young men who liked to take a morning dip in the river stark naked should do so before eight o'clock. He thought it would save embarrassment, he said, because young ladies were not expected to be up and about before that hour.

Other writers followed and a steady flow of books and magazine articles increased the popularity of the waterways. Train travel offered quick and easy access and by the turn of the century Broadland had been well and truly 'discovered'.

Around the time that Davies' handbooks appeared, John Loynes, a carpenter and boatbuilder, began hiring his boat to friends. This developed into a hire business operated from his boatyard at Wroxham. Some of the trading wherries were converted to provide luxury floating accommodation while yet more were purpose-built with bath, kitchen, piano and wind-up gramophone provided.

Perhaps it's true to say that no town has experienced such a dramatic change in its fortunes and its character as Great Yarmouth. At the time of the Norman Conquest there were about 400 people living on the spit of sand – the Denes – making their living by catching herrings.

Thanks to the herring the town prospered and in medieval times it provided a sizeable proportion of the king's navy. At the start of the First World War about a thousand fishing boats claimed Great Yarmouth as their home port.

It is said that the red herring was discovered by chance when a fisherman hung his surplus catch in the roof. The smoke from his fires turned the herrings red and much to his delight he found that they kept for months. Be that as it may, so important was the herring to the prosperity of the town that three tail ends of the 'silver darlings' appear on Great Yarmouth's coat of arms. The red herring has also given us a term much loved and used by writers of detective stories. A smoked and salted red herring drawn across the path of a fox was said to put the hounds off the scent and that's how the term 'red herring' meaning a false trail or dead end came into the language.

When Daniel Defoe came to Yarmouth around 1720 he thought it infinitely superior to Norwich. He said the river afforded it 'the finest quay in England, if not in Europe, not inferior even to that of Marseilles itself. The ships ride here so close that for half a mile one may walk from ship to ship as on a floating bridge all along the shore-side.' He also noted that people living along the coast had another 'harvest' from the sea. He was surprised to see that just about every barn, shed, stable, fence, hogsty and what he called 'necessary-house' was built of the washed up planks and timbers of wrecked ships.

With the rise of tourism and the decline of the fishing

industry, Great Yarmouth experienced a shift away from the riverside to the seaside on the eastern side of the peninsula. 'The fine air of this watering place, the extensive sea view, and its splendid and safe sands, render this town one of the most favoured of seaside resorts,' was how it was described on the eve of the First World War.

Great Yarmouth had become a town Daniel Defoe would not have recognised. His description of the town two hundred years earlier had painted a very different picture. 'It is a very well-governed town,' he said, 'and I have no where in England observed the Sabbath-Day so exactly kept, or the breach so continually punished as in this place. Among all these regularities, it is no wonder if we do not find abundance of revelling, or that there is little encouragement to assemblies, plays, and gaming meetings.' And he was pleased to note that the ladies of the town matched those of neighbouring counties in 'beauty, breeding and behaviour.'

The proximity of the coast to the rivers and broads is both an advantage and a threat. On one hand the variety of facilities and attractions offered by the seaside town and villages coupled with those of Broadland, give the tourist plenty of holiday choices. On the other hand, the sea poses a threat that could change much of the landscape we see today. The Norfolk coastline is constantly changing and over the centuries several villages have disappeared beneath the tides of the North Sea. With global warming and rising sea levels a reality, the threat from the sea is now greater than ever.

One benefit enjoyed by this part of England and one remarked on by a writer a century after Dan Defoe came this way is the healthy climate. He declared, 'The climate, considering the contiguity of this county to the ocean, is more healthful, serene and mild than might be expected. The air of Norfolk is peculiarly salubrious and pleasant. With respect to its climate, its population, its trade and commerce, the character of its inhabitants, the diversified beauties of prospect which embellish it, or especially with respect to the improved state of agriculture, Norfolk may with propriety be denominated THE GLORY OF ENGLAND.'   [His capitals not mine.]

Burgh Castle near Great Yarmouth, Norfolk

Treachery by Moonlight

Iwould hazard a guess and say that if all the old stories about hauntings around England were true, then the most common sort of ghost is probably a monk. That is a little surprising because the country has not exactly been teeming with live monks for several hundreds of years.

Perhaps the answer is that when that nasty tyrant and wife-killer, Henry VIII, abolished the old monasteries back in the 1530s, many of the once great buildings were allowed to become roofless ruins. And there's no better place to set a spooky tale than in the stark and lonely ruins of an old abbey with scary spectres in long black habits and hoods wandering around the place in the moonlight.

Broadland's oldest monastery, the Benedictine abbey of St Benet's at Holm, has its own tale of death and double-dyed treachery involving men in long black habits and hoods as well as men in armour with swords and spears. It is claimed that the monastery was founded around about the year 800 by a small group of monks led by one Suneman. They wanted to get away from the world and they found the peace and isolation they wanted on a small island called Cow Holm set amid wetlands. Today the ruined remains stand beside the River Bure and they are not far from where the Ant and the Thurne come flowing into the Bure from the north. But it was different when the monks first came because in those days the Ant flowed west to east to the north of the monastery site and into the Thurne. Monks often established their houses on islands set in damp, cold and rather unhealthy places – Glastonbury and Ely are two other examples.

Some 70 years later the Vikings came rampaging through the land and their dastardly deeds included the killing of King

Edmund and the destruction of St Benet's. A hundred years or so passed and the abbey was re-established around the year 1000. When King Cnut stamped his authority on England and put an end to many years of war, one of the things he did was to be a patron of the abbey. As we know from the episode of Cnut and his failure to halt the in-coming tide, Cnut was a king who did not always believe everything he was told. There is an old tale that when he heard that the monks of St Benet's had been doing things they should not have done, he put on a disguise and went to see for himself.

When he arrived he was surprised to be met by the sight of the monks all lined up to greet him. 'How did you know I was coming?' asked the king.

'Ah,' said the abbot, 'an angel told me you would come this way and show great generosity to our poor house.' Well, after that the king could not do anything except be generous to the monks, could he? Whatever the truth of the early days of St Benet's, the abbey certainly did prosper in the years to come.

But the story of treachery at the abbey is set at the time of the Norman Conquest. William the Conqueror won his famous victory at the Battle of Hastings on October 14, 1066. [The battle wasn't really fought at Hastings. It was fought six miles up the road at a place where William built Battle Abbey to commemorate his victory in what we call the Battle of Hastings.] Those ruthless Normans soon set about grabbing country estates for themselves and they weren't that fussy about what the English owners had to say about it.

But there were people still prepared to fight the invaders, and one of them was abbot Ethelwold of St Benet's. He was the third abbot of the monastery since its second foundation and he and his predecessor Thurstan had busily replaced the old wooden walls and buildings with new ones of stone. So by the time the Normans arrived Ethelwold was the master of an abbey that was also very much a military stronghold.

Through the winter months of January and February, and into a cold and bleak March the Normans did their best to take the abbot's fortress, but every attack was beaten back. Sometimes the soldiers did not even get close to the walls as they floundered and wallowed in the mud. And when they did get near the walls the abbot and his militant monks and their English retainers beat them off.

So the Normans sent a new man to take charge. His name was Roger Bigod and he came from Calvados in Normandy. He took one look at the situation and decided on a change of tactics. He concluded that where brute force had failed some Calvados cunning might win the day. Under a flag of truce, he sent a messenger to the abbot offering to negotiate an end to the violence. Safe within his walls, Abbot Ethelwold agreed – he could afford to play the waiting game - and soon messages were going back and forth between the abbey and the Norman camp at the end of the causeway at Horning.

The abbot chose as his messenger and intermediary a monk who had been at the abbey for twenty years or more. His name was Wulfric and everyone from the abbot down considered him to be an excellent choice. Down the years he had been meticulous in his duties, he had faithfully observed his vows, and never had he shown a spark of independence or recalcitrance or bad temper. But perhaps because their lives often depended on it, some rough tough warriors like Roger have an instinct that can detect a flaw in a man's character or the duplicity hidden behind a smile.

Roger Bigod was just such a man and he detected in Wulfric something that no other man did. At their meetings he studied his speech and his demeanour; he listened to the tones in his voice and he looked him straight in the eye. The result was that he became more and more convinced that within this black-clad monk, beneath the apparent controlled and calm exterior, there was a smouldering fire of bitterness and suppressed anger.

He cultivated the monk's comradeship with a friendly voice and flattering words, with fresh meats and new-baked bread, with honey cakes and fine wines. The monk thanked his host most gratefully and tucked into all that was put before him with an appetite worthy of a man twice his size. He said that there was no shortage of supplies in the abbey, enough for months of siege in fact, but the truth of the matter was that the fare was becoming monotonous. And being thrown into such lengthy close proximity with his brethren and all the unwashed servants and retainers was proving to be a trial of everyone's patience and tolerance. Therefore the knight would understand why a lowly monk lingered so long in his camp and indulged himself so voraciously at the well-stocked table.

Soon the monk's grumblings became less general and more specific. He had served the abbey long and well. He had been as meticulous in observing the Rule of St Benedict in each and every aspect of prayer and devotion, learning and labour. But within community life there were tensions and conflicts. Some were favoured more than others. Some were preferred above others. And now the politicking of this new abbot had brought conflict and war to the door of the abbey. Many of the Brothers had little stomach for this fight. They wanted a quick return to their ordered life of prayer and the servants had no wish to end their days on the point of a Norman spear.

'But this conflict can soon be ended, and without bloodshed too,' said Roger. 'Remove this obstinate abbot and the problem is solved.'

'Remove Brother Abbott?' said Wulfric.

'Yes, remove him and replace him with a man more fitted for such high office.'

'Where could you find such a man?' asked Wulfric.

'He is here with me, eating my meat and drinking my wine...'

'But we are the only ones here.'

'True,' said Roger, 'and I have always preferred a helmet to a mitre.'

'Me? Do you mean me?' spluttered Wulfric in surprise and indignation. But both his surprise and indignation were as false and hypocritical as was the smile of friendship and generosity that curled upon Roger's lips.

'Together we can end this conflict,' said the Norman knight softly and slowly. 'Help me and I promise that I shall raise you higher than any man living within that abbey. Higher even than you would ever expect from a friend.'

And so the pact of betrayal was agreed.

For his part, Wulfric would open the gates when the Brothers were at Matins, the first service of the day, in the cold, bleak, black hours of the early morning, and when the sentries would be bleary-eyed for want of sleep.

For his part, Roger would see that Abbot Ethelwold was removed from office, and that removal would be permanent. Perhaps the abbot would meet with an unfortunate accident or perhaps he might be unwise enough to resist the lawful commands of armed and armoured agents of the king.

The date was fixed for two days hence, March 21, the feast day of the founder of the Rule, St Benedict.

An hour after midnight Roger and his men gathered in silence at the head of the causeway. No horses had they to carry them. No flaming torches had they to light the way. Yes, the moon was nigh on full, but its light was erratic and fitful.

A wind from the sea sent silver-edged clouds racing across its face and when the light faded the soldiers muttered oaths and curses as they slipped and slithered in the cloying mud.

Wulfric lay in his bed, his imagination plucking thoughts and images from his brain and tossing them back and forth through the tunnels of his mind. He, like the abbey, was wrapped in black silence, and he hated it.

He rose earlier than his fellows and with the furtive and bent-backed stealth of a conspirator he made his way through the abbey church and out into the cloister. Then it was on again, passing the abbot's spacious lodging – a lodging furnished soft and warm that would soon be his own. He skirted round the storehouses and the fishponds, and gratefully vanished into the shadow of the gatehouse.

As he stood shrouded within the deep black shadow he could feel his heart thumping within his chest. Fear was the omnipotent master of his mind and his body shook from his tonsured head to the tips of his ice-cold toes.

He fought for control of his mind. He would be strong. The prize was worth the effort. Why should he have any fear? No sentry had challenged him. No sound had invaded his ears other than that of the soft breeze shaking the reeds and skating across the surface of the river. He breathed deep and his panic drained out of him.

He stared through the spy-hole in the gate.

'Where are they? Why are they not here? They should be here!' The words sped through his brain and he stared again. He detected a glint of moonlight on a spearpoint. Then it was gone. Perhaps his eyes were playing him false? Then he saw a flash of silver light reflected by the hammered iron rim of a shield. Then another from the blade of an unsheathed sword. Yes, they were coming.

He breathed deep once more and heaved up the beam that

barred the gate. He pulled and the hinges squealed in objection to the dead-of-night disturbance. In truth the noise was little more than a sigh, but in Wulfric's ears it was as loud as a thunderclap.

Within moments Wulfric found himself caught up in a whirlpool of pandemonium. Armed men rushed past him, their deep-throated war cries assailing his ears. The sleeping sentries yelled back their consternation at the sudden and successful invasion. So complete was the surprise that not one sword was raised, or one arrow shot in defence of the abbey. No doubt most of the defenders were pleased that it was all over and they still had their lives.

The Normans speedily secured their victory and, as Roger had promised, there had been little bloodshed. Killing peasants and recalcitrant monks would have been a pointless activity - who would then guide the ploughs or pray for the souls of men, even for the souls of fighting men?

Of Abbot Ethelwold there was no sign. He had slipped away through the postern at the other end of the abbey precinct and taken ship for foreign parts.

The clamour subsided. Flaming torches pierced the darkness of the night with fiery light. Victorious Roger Bigod approached Wulfric, now riding on the back of the former abbot's biggest and whitest stallion. With him marched a troop of soldiers and close behind them came the monks of St Benet's, walking two-by-two in an orderly file, eyes down, and chanting a psalm.

'Wulfric!' barked Roger. 'Stand forward! It is time for you to have your reward.'

The chanting stopped. Wulfric allowed a smile of satisfaction to spread across his face and he rubbed his arms in an effort to expel the early morning chill from his bones.

'These are for you,' said Roger and at the wave of his hand

three soldiers stepped forward. One placed a thick and much decorated cope about his shoulder. Another placed a mitre upon his head. The third thrust a staff into his hands.

Roger turned to the silent monks. 'See, Brothers of St Benet's, I present to you your new abbot.' There were some faint murmurs of surprise, even objection. Certainly there was no spontaneous chorus of celebration. Roger turned again to Wulfric and said, 'Abbot Wulfric, see, I have kept my word...' He paused and the silence was heavy before he resumed. 'See, I have kept my promise to you in every detail.'

Wulfric nodded in agreement and before he could utter a syllable of thanks or appreciation Roger added, 'Every detail except one. And now that last detail shall be delivered. As I promised you shall be raised higher than any man in this place.'

At another signal from Roger a rope was thrown from the top of the gatehouse and one end of it smacked the ground at Wulfric's feet. He looked down in horror and a stifled cry escaped his lips as he turned as pale as the moonlight.

A blow on the back of his head knocked him to his knees. He struggled to rise but felt strong hands grasp his arms. He could not move. A noose was pulled over his head and tightened so pitilessly that he felt its fibres burn into his neck. Out of the corner of his eye Wulfric saw Roger raise and drop his hand in another signal. Instantly he was pulled off his feet. His hands pulled at the rope around his neck as he gasped for breath. His eyes bulged from his head. His feet trod upon nothing more substantial than the thin night air.

So ended the brief reign of Abbot Wulfric.

By a twist of fate that few could have foreseen, Abbot Ethelwold won the new Norman king's favour and returned to his abbey after a brief exile in Denmark. He died in 1089 having outlived William the Conqueror by two years.

Roger Bigod went on to even bigger and better things. He was granted estates forfeited by another Norman warlord who got involved in a conspiracy against King William. When the Domesday Book was compiled to find out who owned what, King William was listed as having 241 holdings large and small in Norfolk and Roger came next with 234. Roger did very well out of the conquest of England, founding a family line of lords who became powerful earls of Norfolk. The Bigods built themselves a castle beside the River Waveney at Bungay and some of them turned out to be very troublesome subjects to later kings of England

The monks of St Benet's Abbey – and there was never more than a couple of dozen of them - must have lived well despite their isolation. The abbey had 65 holdings in Norfolk so the monks' pantry should have been well stocked all the year round. St Benet's was attacked again 1381 during the Peasants' Revolt and the abbot was forced to burn lots of old documents. But the real object of the attack failed. The rebels had heard that the bishop of Norwich, Henry Despenser, was there. Unfortunately for them he wasn't. The fighting bishop was busy collecting an army and he eventually caught up with the rebels at North Walsham. The rebels were defeated in a bloody battle and that put an end to the rising in Norfolk.

Strictly speaking, St Benet's escaped dissolution. At the command of the fat and ever-avaricious Henry VIII, the last abbot became the new of bishop of Norwich and was granted the abbey and its estates. The estates and revenues once enjoyed by the bishops of Norwich went to the crown. You can guess who came off best in that deal. So to this day the bishop of Norwich is also the abbot of St Benet's.

As for poor Wulfric it seems he hasn't totally vanished from history. Some people say the spectre of the ambitious Benedictine monk of St Benet's is seen occasionally when the moon is full. Some say he is seen hanging from the end of a rope only once a year late in May. Others assert that the scary sight is to be seen in the early hours of March 21, the old St Benedict's day.

About a mile and a half away to the east of the ruins of St Benet's is Thurne's little thatched church dedicated to St Edmund. In the west wall of the tower is a hole that from the inside points straight at the ruins of St Benet's. Some say it is a 'squint' that allowed lepers outside to see the altar inside the church. But usually squints are holes through pillars or walls inside a church. Another explanation is that it was used to send signals to the abbey when danger threatened. Whatever its true purpose it was being used as a bird's nest when I was there! Back in Norman times Thurne was a small out-of-the-way place. And guess who the two landlords were – yes, that's right, the abbot of St Benet's and Roger Bigod!

Back in medieval times there were lots of institutions big and small run by the monks and nuns and friars of the various orders. Among them were hospitals which by modern standards provided the most basic care service imaginable. Abbot Daniel of St Benet's established a hospital for men and women along the causeway on the way to Horning. But we should remember that medieval hospitals were not only intended to be places where sick people might seek a remedy. They also served as places of shelter for the very old and the very poor, and there were some specifically set aside for people afflicted by leprosy and infectious diseases. The leper houses at Norwich and Yarmouth were sited outside the walls, and there were others across the county in out-of-the-way places. They were often called lazar houses after Lazarus, the much-diseased beggar who sat at a rich man's gate in one of the parables in the New Testament.

For those sailing up the River Bure there isn't much in the

way of habitation once you've left Great Yarmouth. Stretching away to the left is the emptiness of the Halvergate Marshes, an area that in Roman times was a tidal estuary. And off to the right is what was then the island of Flegg. Here there are lots of villages whose names ending in 'by' indicate the lasting influence of the Norsemen from years long ago – Clippesby, Hemsby, Mautby, Rollesby, Thrigby, Scratby and several more.

It's around one hundred miles from north London to the Broads. Back in the 1960s in the days before motorways and dual carriageways were so common, it could take several hours to make the trip, particularly if you got caught in traffic in one of the bottleneck towns along the A11. But the Broads can be so compelling and fascinating for some people that they just have to keep coming back. That was the case with John Smith [not his real name] an amiable and not over ambitious young man who worked for a major banking firm.

He discovered the Broads while on holiday with friends when a young man. They had hired a cruiser for a week at Wroxham and decided that Great Yarmouth might offer some amusement and perhaps female companionship. It was well into Saturday afternoon when they reached the boatyard so they only got as far as Horning before deciding to call it a day. Anyway, their map indicated that there were no more pubs before Acle Bridge.

The next day they set course for the more brash and raucous delights of Great Yarmouth. The weather was good so they took it in turns to take the wheel while the other stretched out in shorts and sunglasses. They had passed Stokesby and John was steering while the others dozed and listened to pop music from Radio Caroline on a transistor radio. And that was when John experienced what he described as 'a presence' for the first time. He heard nothing and saw nothing. The only sensation he detected was a feeling of being watched. That, of course, is not an uncommon sensation for lots of people. Often it happens and there is, indeed, someone watching you or staring in your direction. But seldom is there anything mysterious or unworldly or supernatural or even malicious about it. Sometimes it's all a mistake.

John thought little more about it. Great Yarmouth provided some gaudy diversion for a day or two and a night or two, and on Thursday they turned the cruiser up-river to head for Wroxham. They were about four miles from Great Yarmouth and again John was at the wheel when he it happened to him again. Again a sensation of being watched, and this time there was the feeling of a cold hand being placed on his shoulder. He was stripped the waist so the 'touch' immediately caused him to turn and look behind him. There was no one there. And that was that. The holiday ended, they went home and John might have forgotten all about it. But a couple of years later he returned to the Broads. Three of the four-man 'crew' were the same. Again they started at Wroxham and again the vote was to head for Great Yarmouth.

John was lazing at the 'sharp end' with his eyes closed and he had no precise idea of where they were – somewhere the Yarmouth side of Thurne Mouth - when he experienced what he described as 'a most unnerving sensation'. Again there was the feeling of being watched. Again something like the touch of a cold hand on the shoulder. But this time the touch had a greater reality about it. It was not a touch that gripped or squeezed, but a touch that seemed to impart a desire for assistance.

Then it was gone. Three or four days later they began to retrace their course up the Bure. John sat in the bow and studied the map. He followed every twist and turn of the river and he waited, half expecting, half dreading, for the touch of that cold hand. It came sure enough. But the touch of the hand was no stronger. It was like the touch of an old man's hand. It lingered longer too, and this time John thought no, he believed that he also heard a soft whisper in his right ear. But if the whisper spoke words he did not understand them. Then after a minute or two touch and whisper and sensation were gone and the cruiser turned into the bend of the river that took it close to the old Stracey Arms mill and the Acle Straight.

John said nothing about it. No one else spoke of it so he concluded that no one else had experienced anything unusual. Back to north London and marriage and working harder and longer to meet the costs of creating a family home. John returned to the River Bure when he could, sometimes just for a long weekend. Always he sailed the same stretch of the Bure and each time he experienced the touch of an unseen presence. The most disturbing part of the phenomenon was that each time the experience grew stronger and more intense, and instead of lasting only a minute or two he felt that someone or something was approaching and standing beside him for five or six minutes. But there was never a feeling of menace or malice, threat or hurt.

It was in the 1980s, about twenty years after the first experience, when John had his first sight of 'the presence'. On the first two occasions it had no real or recogniable form. In colour it was brown and grey, and both those colours were dull and pale, its shape blurred and ill defined. John came back to the Bure three times the next year. And three times the year after that. And it was toward the end of a fine day in May that he saw and heard and recognised 'the presence' for what it really was.

First came the feeling of being watched, then the soft touch of a cold hand that had no great strength or power in the fingers. He was about to turn to see what was behind him when he saw a figure on the left bank. It was an old man, one hand leaning on a stick.

His clothes were ridiculous. A brown woollen cap without a peak was perched upon a head that obviously had few hairs. A shirt that had once been as grey as woodsmoke now stained and wet beneath the chin. It had a hole at the left elbow, and about his legs hose that were ill-fitting at the thighs and loose at the hips. He had a stubble beard that was struggling to emerge from a face wrinkled by age and manual toil. His lips moved but John could not hear the words that were spoken.

John steered his boat closer to the bank. The apparition watched and raised a hand. Was he trying to make contact? Was it a greeting or a caution? John reached forward too and he believed that he could feel the cold and bony fingers of the old man grasp his own, but weakly. Then he heard a stronger sound, an insistent sound. The sound was that of a voice but the tone was strange and the word harsh and sharp. Perhaps it was a name.

The sound did not come from the old man because he turned his head and raised the hand that held the stick. The old man took three or four paces, stopped and turned back towards John. He waved the hand that held no stick and removed the cap for a few moments. The sensation of the touch on the shoulder and the soft grip of the hand faded from John's senses. The whispers ceased. Once more the old man turned away from John. Two or three steps and the image began to fade. Two or three more and the old man was gone.

John returned to the Broads later that year, and the next year, and the next. But he never saw the old man again. Never again did he experience that unnerving feeling of being watched or of a cold and bony hand touching his shoulder. He asked himself questions. Why had no one else spoken of seeing the old man? Had no one else seen what he had seen?

Why had the apparation become stronger and more distinct over time only for it to vanish when it was at its plainest?

He visited the friends who had been with him on those early cruises. He hinted at something strange having happened. Had they felt anything? A chuckled denial then laughter was the response in every case. So, he had been the only one to experience 'the presence'. He started to read books about ghosts and hauntings. He went to spiritualist meetings, and he even consulted a couple of mediums. He concluded that an awful lot of rubbish has been written on the subject, much of it contradictory and much of it aimed at the gullible.

He learned that it was quite common for only one or two people in a group to experience the presence of a ghost. He also learned that cynics down the centuries had used precisely that fact as an argument against the existence of ghosts. For a time John questioned himself. Had he really felt and seen what he thought he had felt and seen? Could not the experiences have been a cumulative series of illusions and daydreams and fancies that had been triggered by him obsessively returning to the same place again and again? He argued the case with himself many times and he concluded that what he thought had happened really did happen.

Then chance took a hand. John, now a widower, retired and he decided to move to a smaller house. The usual problems of 'downsizing' came to the surface – too much furniture for a smaller house and far too much stuff stored away in the garage and the loft after decades of family life. He found things he had not seen for years – old books and gramophone records, old photographs and children's toys, old clothes and boxes of bits and bobs kept simply because they might come in handy one day. And in an old shoe box he found his old diaries.

John had kept a diary for most of his life but had stopped the day his wife died. They were not detailed chronicles of events and conversations. They were just cursory notes of where he had been and what he had done. Typical of the terse entries were 'Thursday March 16 1978 Work. Routine day. Cold. Glad to get home' and 'Friday November 13 1981 Flu. In bed all day.'

He flicked through the pages and mental pictures of faces and places came flooding back. He had recorded his last sighting of the spectral old man in just six words. 'Sunday May 20, 1984. Broads. Saw the 'old man' again.' Of course John did not know at that time that it was to be the last sighting.

He was about to put the lid on the box when he paused, had a 'brainwave' and began searching for his diaries from the early 1960s. What he was looking for was not in 1960. Nor in 1961. He found it under Sunday May 20 1962 - 'Broads holiday. A strange experience. To Great Yarmouth.' Why had his experiences of the old man begun and apparently ended on the same day, May 20?

What was special about May 20? It was the day the Spanish Armada set sail in 1588. It was the day the foundation stone of the Royal Albert Hall was laid in 1867. It was the opening day of the first Chelsea Flower Show in 1913, and the day the Americans tested their first H bomb at Bikini Atoll in 1956. John moved to a new home in Suffolk and once he had settled in the coincidence of May 20 began to exercise his mind. It was a puzzle he was determined to solve.

He began looking into the history of Broadland and the River Bure. He followed many trails and most of them went nowhere. Then he found references to an institution that had been part college and part hospital-almshouse. It was called 'God's House of Herringby [Collegii de Heringby voc

Goddeshouse]. The benefactor was one Hugh atte Fenne, a wealthy 15th century merchant, who had established it for a master, three priests, two servants and eight poor men. Under the terms of Hugh's will there were also distributions of alms to the poor of Yarmouth.

But what caught John's attention was the church dedication – it was to St Ethelbert, a king of East Anglia who lived about half a century before the more famous St Edmund. Ethelbert was still a teenager when he was murdered while on a visit to King Offa of Mercia. Ignoring the warnings of his mother, Ethelbert had gone to seek marriage with Offa's daughter. But instead of coming home with a bride, Ethelbert was murdered at Offa's command as part of a political power struggle. Down the years, most of the blame has been assigned to the treacherous machinations of Offa's wife, Cynethryth. According to one version of the assassination she arranged it so that when the young king sat on his chair a trap door opened and he fell into a cellar below where the nasty queen's servants were waiting to kill him. In medieval times Ethelbert was venerated as a martyr and his cult was particularly popular in East Anglia.

The connection was May 20, the date of the murder of Ethelbert and the date on which his feast was celebrated. Like many medieval hospitals, 'God's House of Herringby' was shut down in Tudor times and sold off to a local bigwig.

But still John was not satisfied. He became convinced there there was more to it than that. He persuaded himself that there must be a link between himself and the spectral old man. He began to investigate his family history, tracing his way back through the generations. Did he ever establish a blood connection? I don't know. And I can't ask him because he died in 2004.

Old Remedies –
but not for the squeamish

Whether you were born rich or poor, whether you were lord of the manor or a muddy, toiling peasant, one thing was for sure about life in the old days and that was that it wasn't much fun being ill or injured.

Mention has been made of St Apollonia who was invoked for toothache and St Roch who was claimed to give protection against the plague. You can see pictures of Apollonia, the patron saint of dentists, on the screens at Ludham and Barton Turf. She is shown holding one of her teeth in a pair of pincers. Pincers are her symbol because she was tortured by having all her teeth pulled out.

Now a brief digression. It seems that medical services had not improved a great deal when some three hundred years after the founding of Herringby hospital, Norfolk's most famous diarist had a touch of the toothache. That diarist was James Woodforde who was a village parson living near Norwich in the late 18th century. In one entry he tells of what happened when he was afflicted by toothache in 1776. 'June 4, My tooth pained me all night; got up a little after five this morning and sent for one Reeves, a man who draws teeth in this parish. About seven he came and drew my tooth, but shockingly bad indeed. He broke away a great piece of my gum and broke one of the fangs of the tooth. It gave me exquisite pain all the day after and my face was swelled prodigiously in the evening, and much pain. Gave him two shillings and sixpence. He is too old, I think, to draw teeth. He can't see very well.'

Mr Woodforde might well have suffered a lot less if he had taken his problem to a Norfolk doctor who was born a few miles away. He was a parson's son who made a name for himself with his rather eccentric treatments. He was Doctor Messenger Monsey and he had a unique way of removing bad teeth and he was so confident in its effectiveness that he used it on himself. No pincers and broken gums for him. He would have the offending tooth out of the patient's head with the speed of a gunshot.

He would tie a strong piece of catgut to the offending molar and the other end he affixed to a bullet. Then he loaded a pistol with a full charge of gunpowder, rammed home the ball and fired. It was reported, 'On the trigger being pulled the operation was performed effectually and speedily. The doctor could only rarely prevail on his friends to permit him to remove their teeth by this original process. Once a gentleman who had agreed to try the novelty, and had allowed the apparatus to be adjusted, at the last moment exclaimed, 'Stop, stop, I've changed my mind!'

'But I haven't and you're a fool and a coward for your pains,' answered the doctor, pulling the trigger. In an instant the tooth was extracted, much to the timid patient's delight and astonishment.' Doctor Monsey's methods seem to have been effective, at least as far as he was concerned because he lived to be 95 years old.

Another method of dealing with health problems in the old days was to go along to the village cunning man or wise woman, cross their palm with silver and see what they had to suggest. Sometimes the authorities would clamp down on these alleged sages because it was often thought they were dabbling in matters that were more akin to witchcraft than dispensing traditional herbal remedies.

Here are some more supposed remedies for toothache from years ago. When next 'the toothache doth wrack the jaw and gums' it was suggested you go along to a churchyard at midnight when the moon was thin [new], dig up a skull and bite a tooth from it. Then keeping the tooth in your pocket, you should go home and write a prayer on a piece of paper. The prayer should also be spoken three times before burning the piece of paper. The promise was that 'the ache shall diminish to nought.'

If you didn't fancy the idea of digging up a skull at midnight you could try going to a graveyard, kneeling on a grave, chewing on a handful of grass and then spitting it out before you swallowed any. Doing that a few times was supposed to ensure you never got toothache again even if you lived to be a hundred.

If that didn't work and you didn't fancy a midnight trip to a graveyard, you might care to try pills made of pepper and the inner rind of an elder tree. Rubbing your gums with a piece of wood taken from a gibbet was supposed to be an effective remedy for toothache as well as having the bonus property of removing warts.

A painless method of tooth extraction that was suggested was to apply powdered newts and beetles to an aching tooth with the fingers of the right hand. If you refrained from spitting it out you could be assured that the tooth would fall out by itself, and painlessly too.

Probably the most bizarre method is this one and it requires no 'physic' at all. So, if you want to go through life without ever feeling so much as a twinge of toothache all you have to do is make sure you always 'dress and undress the left leg and the left foot before the right'.

As well as Apollonia for toothache and Roch for plague and pestilence, there was a long list of saints who could be invoked for protection against other dangers and diseases.

St Agatha, the patron saint of nurses, could be called upon by women when they were troubled by sore breasts and she also defended your house against 'fire and fearful flame'. St Clara was good for sore eyes and St Margaret was another favourite with women because she could be called on for protection against the dangers of childbirth. Women who were fed up with their husbands could appeal to St Wilgefortis [also known as Uncumber].

There was St Laurence for back problems; Petronilla and Genevieve were invoked against a variety of fevers which often went under the name of the dreaded quartan ague. Calling upon Benedict was thought to be good for stones in the kidney and bladder, and Genow was good for gout

Then there were Blaise who protected against bones sticking in the throat, and Gertrude who was said to rid the house of mice and kill all the rats. Vitus was good for pacifying the 'raging minds of furious folks', and Erasmus soothed 'the colic and the griping of the guts'. Gregory helped little boys to learn the alphabet and become good scholars, and Nicholas was the patron saint of mariners and was said to keep them safe from danger when they were 'beaten by boisterous waves and tossed in dreadful seas'. Nicholas was also claimed as patron saint by pawnbrokers, apothecaries, perfume makers, unmarried women and even thieves. And his patronage of children has resulted in the Christmas cult of Santa Claus.

There was Martin for heavy drinkers, Leonard was for locksmiths and prisoners, and Louis of wig makers. Priests had their own patron in Thomas.

Winifred was the patroness of virgins while Thomas Becket looked after eunuchs. Osyth, another East Anglian saint, was another one who appealed to women because she helped to keep the household keys safe and sound. Ethelbert gave protection against thieves and Anne could be asked to help when things were lost. Loy was the protector of horses,

Hubert, the patron saint of hunters, could be called upon in hope of relief by those bitten by a mad dog. Crispin was the patron of travelling shoemakers and Gallus looked after the interests of geese keepers. Doctors, surgeons and philosophers claimed Cosmas and Damian as their patron saints. And so the list went on.

One of the most popular saints in the days when church walls were covered with painted pictures was a veritable giant of a man. He was usually to be seen painted on the wall opposite the porch and door into the church. And the reason he was so popular was because it was believed that whoever saw his image would not die that day.

The saint's name was Christopher and he is the patron saint of travellers. There was a time when every traveller had his image around his neck and every motorist had a 'St Christopher' on his car-key ring. Christopher's image can still be seen on the walls of several churches in and around Broadland. He is usually shown as a giant wading through a river with Christ as a child on his shoulder.

Christopher – the name means Christ-bearer – was said to have been a large and fearsome looking man who decided to serve the Devil. But when he discovered that the Devil feared Christ he changed his allegiance. A hermit instructed him in religion and told him to help travellers across a dangerous river. One day a child asked his help to cross a river. The child was placed on Christopher's shoulder, but as he advanced Christopher found his burden getting heavier and heavier. It was a real struggle for him to get to the other side of the river.

'Child, you put me in great peril. I don't think I could carry a heavier load!' said Christopher when at last he gained the far bank. The child's reply was that Christopher should not be surprised at the weight of his burden because he had 'borne all the world on his shoulders, and its sins also.' Believers also invoked St Christopher against river hazards, plague and sudden death.

If invoking the saints failed to help people could always turn to the local wise woman or cunning man. They were usually elderly men or women whose experience and knowledge of folk medicine gave them considerable knowledge of the healing properties of plants and herbs. But in the days when being accused of witchery could bring you to the gallows, these local practitioners of traditional medicine were often called white witches to distinguish them from the supposedly more malevolent ones who followed the Devil.

Broadland abounds with wildlife – birds, mammals, insects and many species of plants. Here are some of the properties attributed to some of those plants by apothecaries and physicians hundreds of years ago and some of the traditions associated with them. [This is not to suggest that they are effective or that you should try them. If you have medical problems you should consult your local doctor.]

One of the most common sights in the middle of the year in Broadland is the purple loosestrife. It was considered to be very good for sore eyes as well as spots and scabs on the skin. Sometimes they were attached to the harness of skittish horses in the hope that the animals would calm down. The cuckoo flower, also called lady's smock, is a wild flower that flowers in April and May. Its leaves were described many years ago as being 'of a blushing white colour'. It was said to be 'excellent good for the scurvy, they provoke urine, and excellently warm a cold and weak stomach, restoring lost appetite, and help digestion.'

Feverfew was thought to be particularly beneficial for women being 'a general strengthener of their wombs, and a remedy for such infirmities as a careless midwife has there caused'. It was also recommended for 'ague-fits' and to take away freckles, spots and deformities of the face. Fried with a little wine and oil in a frying pan and applied warm it was supposed to help with 'wind and colic in the lower part of the belly'. One 17th century physician who also put great faith in astrology also praised it as 'an especial remedy against opium taken too liberally'.

To break the kidney stone and help you get rid of it from your body the common marsh pennywort was suggested. A small dose of dried and powdered primrose was claimed to be effective for nervous disorders. Wild valerian was suggested as a medicine that would 'frequently loosen the bowels when other purgatives have proved ineffectual'. It was also proposed for nervous affections such as inveterate headaches, tremblings, palpitations of the heart, vapours and hysteric complaints.

A syrup made with water lilies was said to 'settle the brain of frantic persons'. One physician reported that the leaves of the water plantain 'are frequently made use of by country people for piles and its juice stops the spitting of blood'. Roots of the yellow water flag were reported as being good for 'resisting putrefaction and useful against pestilential contagions and corrupt noxious air'.

Here are some more potions and prescriptions from the time of Oliver Cromwell.

To take away little red pimples from the face take two ounces of lemon juice, two ounces of rosewater, a pinch of silver supplement, mix them into an ointment and rub your face with the same at going to bed and when you get up in the morning rub your face with fresh butter and rub the same clean off. Or dissolve camphire in vinegar and mix it with celandine water and wash the face with it; this cured a maid in twenty days that had been troubled with the infirmity half so many years.

To expel the faints, swoons and giddies in maidens. Maidens are oft afflicted with strange swimmings, swoonings and giddy romantic notions much to the neglect of their duties and chores. A decoction made with the flowers of lavender, the syrup of horehound, fennel, asparagus root and a little cinnamon is very profitably used to help giddies and turnings of the brain. All wise and good housewives hold in their larder close-stoppered bottles of the decoction of rosemary in weak wine to calm all cold diseases of the head and the brain, and also the giddiness or swimming drowsiness or dullness of the mind that is like to a stupidness.

The people in the northern regions of this realm give milk in which roots of barrenwort have been boiled to the females of the domestic animals when they run after the males and they say it has the certain effect of stopping the natural emotions. They have from this been taught to give it to young women of robust habits who are subject to violent hysteric complaints with good success. They give it as a decoction of the root made strong and sweetened. It is said that if they take it in too large quantity it renders them stupid for some hours but no ill consequence has attended this.

For the French pox. Distilled water of hounds' tongue herb and root is good to wash sore places for it heals all manner of wounds and foul ulcers that arise from the French pox. Amaranthus, also called flower-gentle, is an excellent qualifier of unruly actions and the passions of Venus. The flowers dried and beaten to powder is a singular remedy for venereal disease. A strong decoction of woodsage or hearts-ease that flower and seed in spring and summer is an excellent cure for the itch, scabs and disorders that come from excess and naughty wantonness in the company of bawds and strumpets. St John's wort is good for this and for those who cannot make their water.

To be rid of a carbuncle. Guinea pepper that is a native of the Indies is of considerable service. Applied with hen's grease it dissolves cold imposthumes and carbuncles. Mixed with vinegar it dissolves hardness of the skin. A plaister of pennyroyal takes away carbuncles and blotches.

How to cause an abatement of an ague. Take as much snuff of a candle as would lie on a sixpence and make into an electuary with honey. Another commended remedy is to take a red earthen pan in which you must place parings of finger and toe-nails together with a lock of hair and a small piece of raw beef. Tie black silk over the pan and bury it in the centre of a wood in ground that has never been broken. As the meat does decay so the fever shall abate. A preservative against the ague is to take pepper and gin while fasting on a Friday morning; another being to consume pills of blackbottle spiders and butter.

To stop the lask also called diarrhoea. Grate Good Friday bread into water and thus it is partaken of as a thick soup. For the best efficiency the bread must be baked and the dough made on Good Friday before sunrise or church-time.

To heal a rupture or rickets of a child. Select a young ash tree and spilt it longitudinally about five feet; the fissure then being kept wide open the naked child is passed through thrice always head foremost. When this operation has been performed the wounded tree is bound up with packthread and as the bark healeth so shall the afflicted child recover.

Dimness of the eye. Juice of rue and fennel with a little honey and the gall of a cock put thereunto helps a dimness of the eyesight.

For stoppages of the liver. Use garden thyme in your drinks and broths to prevent stoppages before they come and to cure them after they are come. Liver of a hare dried and beaten to powder cures all diseases of the liver in man.

For sore breasts. A handful of figs stamped till the kernels be broken, tempered with fresh grease of hog, applied to the breast as warmly as may be endured presently takes away the anguish.

An essence for headaches. Headaches are sometimes caused by an obnoxious vapour ascending out of the stomach. For common headaches take of French brandy or rectified spirit of wine one quart; put it into a strong bottle and add one ounce of camphire cut small, a quarter of an ounce of the essence of lemon and two ounces of the strongest volatile spirit of sal ammoniac. Stop the bottle close and shake it three or four times a day for a week. The method of using it is to rub the hand with a little of it and hold it upon the part afflicted until it is dry. If the pain is not quite relieved repeat it till it is.

A remedy for aches and pains in the bones, limbs and joints. Take friar's balsam and tincture of myrrh, of each one ounce, spirits of turpentine two ounces, and old strong ale dregs three ounces, mix well together and bathe the afflicted part of the body.

A cure for the piles and sores. Eat rosemary and sage with bread and butter and apply wheat flour and honey by way of a plaister. The green herb of catmint bruised and applied to the fundament and lying there for two or three hours easeth the pains of the piles.

To loosen the binding of the belly. White beet loosens the belly and is of a cleansing and digesting quality to provoke urine. Flowers of the peach steeped all night in a little wine standing warm, strained forth in the morning and drank fasting does gently open the belly and move it downward.

How to kill worms or bot-worms in the body. Take half a glass of brandy and put therein as much fine sulphur as will lay upon a shilling and mix. Burn a bread crust in fire till black. Chew in your mouth for five minutes after which time put it out again and immediately take the medicine early in the morning.

How to cure warts, freckles and knots. To banish warts pass the hand of a dead body on three successive days over the parts afflicted If this fail go into a field and take a black snail and rub the warts with the same nine times one way and nine times another and stick the snail upon a blackthorn and the warts shall waste away. A black snail will also cure corns being lain thereon as a plaster. If you have bleeding warts take a piece of raw beef that never had any salt and rub them with the same in the same manner as you used the snail above mentioned, bury the piece of beef in the earth. Another remedy to rid the flesh of warts commended by some is to cut the initial letter of your Christian and surnames into the bark of an ash tree when it has keys. Count the number of warts that afflict you and cut a notch for each one and as the bark grows the warts shall go. Wheatmeal boiled in vinegar helps shrinking of the sinews and heals freckles, spots and pimples on the face. Wheatmeal applied with salt takes away hardness of the skin, warts and hard knots in the flesh.

To repel an invasion of rheumatism. Constantly wear a galvanic ring which is a ring of silver into which a piece of copper has been let into the inside, on the longest finger of the right hand. This constant contact aided by moisture of the hand will maintain a continual galvanic current to alleviate or remove all rheumatisms.

For a black eye. Flour of beans and fenugreek mixed with honey and rose leaves and the white of an egg applied to the eyes helps them that are swollen or do water or have received a blow upon them if used with wine.

For the Plague. Seeds or leaves of blue-bottle, called also

hurt-sickle because it turns the edges of sickles that reap corn, taken in wine is good against plague and all such diseases. They grow in cornfields and if you please to take them from thence and transplant them in your garden, especially towards the full of the moon, they shall grow more than double they are and change colour.

Sometimes as well as suggesting a herbal remedy, the cunning man or wise woman would propose that certain words or actions of a religious character should be added, and perhaps even a prayer. Then the local authorities in both Church and State were likely to take an interest in their activities. Witchcraft was a heresy but in England it was the responsibility of the civil authorities to pursue it as a criminal offence. Here are some of those questionable cures that relied heavily on superstition and old wives' tales.

To banish an ague take early in the morning a dose of elixir and hang three spiders about your neck and your ague shall be driven away. Otherwise wear about your neck a piece of a nail taken from a cross and wrapped in wool, or drink wine wherein a sword that has drawn blood has been dipped three hours. Otherwise let the urine made by the sick body early in the morning be softly heated nine days until it all be consumed into vapour. Otherwise pare the nails of one that has an ague, put them into a linen cloth and tie about the neck of a live eel and set the same eel into water and the ague shall be abated. Otherwise let the patient make three crosses with white chalk on the back of the kitchen chimney, a large one in the middle and a smaller one on each side. And as the smoke of the fire covers them so shall the ague disappear. A charm for the ague is to be said up the chimney by the eldest female of the family. She must say, 'Tremble and go! First day shiver and burn. Tremble and quake! Second day shiver and learn. Tremble and die! Third day never return.'

For faints and fits take the sick man by the hand and whisper these words softly in his ear, 'I conjure you by the sun and the moon that you rise and fall no more.' Otherwise drink in the night spring water out of a skull of one that has been slain or eat a pig killed with a knife that slew a man. If a young woman has fits she must obtain from eleven unmarried men a small piece of silver, either a piece of a broken spoon, buckle, brooch or a coin. These pieces are to be taken to a worker in metal who forms of them a ring which is to be worn by the person afflicted on the fourth finger of the left hand. If the sufferer be a man his relief comes from the liberality of the same number of maidens.

To cure fits take sliver of lead from a church window and wear next to the skin in an amulet or cut three pieces of lead of the size of a half-farthing from different spouts on the south side of a church. If a husband or lover takes scrapings from the diamond panes of a window on the south side of a church and fashions an ornament that has the shape of a heart it shall cure the sore breasts of the woman he loves if she shall wear it constantly.

A flayed mouse roasted or powdered and drunk all at one time perfectly helps such as cannot hold their water, especially if it be used three days. To banish a cough do one of these. For the chin cough drink spring water from a silver chalice. Otherwise give the sufferer a live frog which they must hold by its head in their mouth. Otherwise hang in a chimney a string of snails which they have passed through their hands. Let the person drink milk which a ferret has lapped or take hairs from the back of a donkey and put them in a bag around the neck.

To be rid of warts rub them with a golden ring or wipe with water on an elder leaf then put the leaf deep in the earth where it may rot and the wart shall dry up anon. Otherwise wash your hands in a polished silver basin wherein there is not a drop of water. Do this by the light of moonbeams only and it shall take away the warts from the hands if it be often done, Otherwise rub them against the flesh of a man that has fathered a red-haired child out of wedlock.

For a crick in the neck wash it well in May Day dew taken from the grave of a young man buried in a churchyard. He that stands a rusty sword at his bedside shall not suffer any cramps in the night. Rub all sprains with the underside of a live toad and soon they shall be gone. He that holds a dying robin in his hand shall ever after have a tremor in that hand and nought can cure it. Blue periwinkle being powdered and taken in wine does renew the vigour of a man to his wife.

For any soreness of the throat touch the place with the hand of one that died an untimely death or let a virgin lay her hand on the sore and say, 'Apollo denies that the heat of the plague can increase where a naked virgin quencheth it.' Then have her spit three times upon it.

If a man suffers a wound caused by a blade or anything that is metal he should burnish that which caused the hurt so that it has no rust. Also he may hasten perfect healing if he rub the wound with that which caused it but only if it be done after sunset and before sunrise. Rain collected in pails and pipkins [small earthenware cooking pots] from a church roof makes an excellent physic for lameness in the legs.

The author who recorded these ridiculous 'cures' added, 'The conjuror who has the intent to deceive and make silly people believe and repose confidence in his words, charms and conjurations is a seducing witch be he called magician, sorcerer, soothsayer, juggler, charmer, star-gazer, figure-caster or astrologer. They are all deceivers of silly people.'

The century or so after 1560 was the main period of witch mania in England, and it often manifested itself in areas where the new religious fundamentalism [Puritanism] was strong and its adherents had their hands on the levers of power.

The mania in East Anglia reached its peak when tensions and conflicts within society were magnified by the political conflict of the Civil War. Matthew Hopkins, the self-styled Witchfinder General, and his accomplices, toured the region in 1645 and 1646 and they were responsible for more than a hundred supposed witches being hanged.

The great majority of the supposed witches who were brought to trial were women, many of them old and virtually destitute. One parson who opposed the witch craze said that it reached such a pitch that virtually every old woman with a squeaky voice, a hairy lip, an old and worn coat on her back, a quarrelsome temper and a scolding tongue, with hardly a tooth left in her head and a cat or dog at her side was not only suspected of being a witch but condemned as one by her neighbours.

In August 1645 Hopkins was invited to search for witches in Yarmouth, the town's civic fathers resolving that 'the gentleman Mr Hopkins being employed in the county for discovering and finding out witches, be sent for to search for such wicked persons, if any be, and have his fee and allowances for his pains, as he has in other places.' One way of detecting witches was to search the suspect's body for places where they were supposed to suckle their imps. The women who carried out this duty were to be paid a shilling a day.

Wherever he went Hopkins usually obliged by finding a suitable number of witches within the community. At Yarmouth sixteen suspects were detained and five or six were hanged. Hopkins told his assistant John Stearne that one of the miscreants had made a clay picture of her intended child victim, stuck a nail in the head and buried it. Stearne wrote, 'I was told by Master Hopkin who was there and took her confession and went to look for the picture and that the child (as I have heard) did soon after mend and grew lusty again. A hellish invention.'

But generally speaking, Norfolk showed little enthusiasm for Hopkins and his crew. His methods were criticised and the fundamental beliefs on which he based his activities were questioned. Hopkins and friends withdrew and concentrated their efforts in Suffolk, Essex and Cambridgeshire.

There was a landmark case in 1662 involving two Lowestoft women who scraped a living by childminding and begging herrings. Rose Cullender and Amy Duny, were charged with bewitching children so that they had fits, saw spectres and vomited pins. It was also said that they had bewitched a farmer's cart, caused a new chimney to collapse and made pigs 'leap and caper and immediately fall down and die'. And when an imp in the shape of a toad was put on a fire it vanished in a flash like exploding gunpowder. Much of the bogus evidence was given by hysterical young girls who had been coached by their parents. Thirty years later it would be used as a model for the notorious Salem witch-hunt in America. The judge had no doubt about the crimes of the women and they were hanged. But in the next few years attitudes changed in England and in 1736 the witchcraft laws were abolished.

But old beliefs die hard. Instead of being objects of compassion, old people 'defaced by infirmity and dotage' were still sometimes seen as malevolent evil-doers, particularly when things went wrong for no apparent reason. And sometimes the results could be quite comic.

One case that was recorded involved a Yarmouth man who fell ill after eating some sausages he had won in a raffle.

'Some friends persuaded him that he was bewitched and advised him to consult Mrs Mortimer, a well-known cunning woman. His mother accompanied him on his visit to this woman, who at first alarmed them by the fierce way she received them. As they made their business known to her, the old woman found that the man was likely to prove a good customer and she very soon cooled down and admitted them.

'The man paid a sovereign and a written copy of a prayer was given to him, and he was ordered to wear this next to his heart, and to take a mixture that the old hag gave him. He was also required to send to her some hair cut from the nape of the neck, parings of his toe and fingernails and a bottle of urine. These were to be operated upon by her in order to complete the cure. The man got better and Mrs Mortimer then demanded another ten shillings, which he refused to pay, but finding himself again in declining health he paid the money, after which he recovered, and continued well till the death of the old hag.'

Another instance concerned a farmer's wife who had lost some feathers and consulted a wise woman about it. When she was assured that they would be found the wife thought she would save herself the fee. 'Provoked by this the prophetess repeated the assurance that the feathers should come back, but added that the owner should not be the better for them. The enquirer, however, fully satisfied that she should recover her goods, laughed at the threat and returned in glee, congratulating herself on having outwitted the witch, and obtained the information so cheaply. As soon as she got home she called her maids to go to milking; and when they had about half done, hearing a slight noise, she raised her head, and saw her feathers come flying into the milking yard like a swarm of bees, and, to her great annoyance, beheld them direct their flight toward the cows, and settle themselves snugly in the half-filled milk pails thus spoiling both milk and feathers. It will readily be imagined that, after this catastrophe, no one ever ventured to defraud Mrs Barrett of her dues.'

Just as there were tenacious old beliefs, traditions and superstitions linked with the names of saints, plants and herbs, and many an old remedy, so there were with notable days of the year.

Twelfth Night was an occasion for merriment. The Twelfth Night king and queen would be the man and woman who found the bean and pea in the plum cake. Years ago it was usual to keep Christmas decorations until early February. Then everything had to be removed by Candlemas Day [February 2]. It was remarked that members of the gentry would send a servant to their local church on Candlemas eve to make sure that there was not a leaf or a berry or a twig on the family pew. If anything did remain it was seen as an omen of a death in the family during the year ahead.

St Agnes' Eve [January 20] was a good time for young women to try to discover who their future husband would be. Two of the ways they could do this was by sticking pins in their sleeves while reciting a prayer or by fasting. They could try again on St Valentine's Day by pinning five bay leaves to their pillow in the hope they would then dream of their heart's desire. Other favoured days were said to be New Year's Eve, St Valentine's Eve or Day, St Mark's Eve [April 24], May Day, Midsummer Day, Halloween, St Catherine's Day [November 25] St Thomas's Eve [December 20] and at Christmas.

Sallow, also called goat willow and palm willow, was used to decorate Broadland churches on Palm Sunday. In parts of Broadland, it was believed to have the power to keep witches at bay like rowan, yew or seven elder trees.

At Midsummer a young woman who lays a clean cloth on the table and puts out bread, cheese and ale, and then sitting there with the front door open will soon meet her intended husband. He will enter, have a drink, bow, fill the glass again, put it on the table, bow once more and leave.

The four quarter days, Lady Day [March 25], Midsummer Day [June 24], Michaelmas Day [September 29] and Christmas Day [December 25] were important days in the calendar and on Michaelmas those who could afford it would celebrate by feasting on a goose – 'At Christmas a capon, at Michaelmas a goose.'

Some days of the year were considered particularly perilous and whatever plan was started would come to no good end. According to old almanacs the unlucky days in January are when the moon is three or four days old. Then there are six days in the year that are 'perilous of death'. These days were January 3, July 1, October 2, April 30, August 1 and the last day of December. The last three were particularly dangerous, so much so that doctors were advised not to bleed their patients because their veins would be full to bursting. And taking a drink within fifteen days or eating a goose within forty days meant you would die. Letting blood in early March from the right arm, and from the left arm in early April would prevent you getting a fever or gout.

The day you cut your toenails or the position of a mole on your body. Even itches and sneezes. They can all tell your fortune. So the next time you cut you toenails you might care to remember this old rhyme -

> Cut them on Monday, cut them for health;
> Cut them on Tuesday, cut them for wealth;
> Cut them on Wednesday, cut them for news;
> Cut them on Thursday, a pair of new shoes;
> Cut them on Friday, cut them for sorrow;

Old Remedies – but not for the squeamish

Cut them on Saturday, love comes tomorrow.
Cut them on Sunday, ill luck all the week.

Back in the days of the Tudors people were eager to know their fate and Queen Elizabeth I went as far as having an astrologer pick a lucky day for her coronation. Another popular way of foretelling fate was by the position of moles on the body. One on your back indicated success in money matters. One near your navel said you would have a big family and one on your bottom indicated a comfortable life. Moles on the left side of the body indicated negative aspects of character and fate. For example, on a man's left shoulder it said he was likely to be selfish and quarrelsome, and on a woman she will turn out to be a sharp-tongued, scolding shrew.

In itchy right elbow meant you'll soon get good news, but the tidings will be bad if it was the left elbow. An itchy nose meant you'll meet a fool before noon and a lover before Sunday. An itch on the lips indicated you'll be kissed by a stranger, on the chin it meant you are heading for a fall, on the right shoulder the burdens of life will ease, on the left shoulder your sorrows multiply. An itch on the palm of your right hand says you'll get rich. On the left hand you'll get into debt. On the back of your hands your wife has a lover. As for sneezes -

Sneeze on Monday, sneeze for danger,
Sneeze on Tuesday, kiss a stranger,
Sneeze on Wednesday, get a letter,
Sneeze on Thursday, something better,
Sneeze on Friday, sneeze for sorrow,
Saturday, see your true love tomorrow.
On Sunday safety seek or it'll be bad
luck all the week.

Time for a Touch of Romance

They say that the course of true love never did run smooth. Well, it certainly didn't for one of the most romantic ghosts of Broadland. In life he had cut a dashing figure – a young man full of life and energy, tall and handsome, and conspicuous in his fine red coat, white breeches and high black cap.

It was the uniform of one of the King George's best regiments of foot that he wore, and William wore it with pride. [We'll call him William because no one knows what his real name was.] It was 1805 and England was at war with France. A year earlier Napoleon had crowned himself Emperor of the French in Paris and during the summer of 1805 he had gathered a huge army at Boulogne ready to mount an invasion of England. He must have had high hopes of victory if only he could get his troops across the English Channel.

England stood as best prepared as it could be with regiments of regulars and militia standing ready to repel any descent on the coast. Quite what their chances would have been against Napoleon's veterans must be a matter for debate. Among the possible targets for a swift descent upon England were the wide and gently sloping beaches of the East Anglian coast. They would be easy targets for an invasion force if only the battleships of Nelson's navy were not in the way.

But in the long warm summer days of that year the plots and politics of invasion had suddenly come to mean very little to William. A new and all-consuming interest had taken command of his thoughts and emotions. And that interest was the pert and pretty young daughter of a well-to-do farmer who lived near Potter Heigham. Her name was Mary Greenacre, and William was not the only handsome young man in uniform or civilian attire to be attracted by the sight of this pretty and personable Norfolk girl.

Whenever he could the inventive and imaginative William would arrange a necessary errand that would require his presence somewhere in the vicinity of farmer Greenacre's home. And sometimes he would be rewarded with a glimpse of Mary, and sometimes he would get the opportunity to exchange a few words. The couple shared a mutual attraction, of that there was no doubt. Their paths would cross with ever-greater frequency. It was always by chance as far as anyone else could tell - at church on Sundays, or during the week when farmer Greenacre took wife and daughter to Stalham or Martham or, as a special treat, to Norwich. Then in August and September it was time to gather in the harvest and many of the soldiers found themselves helping with the task. William was one of those detailed to help at the Greenacre farm.

The shortening days of October and November made it more difficult for the young couple to meet. The opportunities for the young couple to enjoy a few minutes together became fewer and rarer until eventually, as was inevitable, their secret was a secret no more. Word of their attachment came to the ears of farmer Greenacre and his anger exploded.

'My daughter shall never marry a soldier!' he declared in fierce and ringing tones. 'My daughter is a silly young thing whose head has been turned by a handsome face and scarlet uniform. And both never were reliable tokens of future prospects or genuine and honourable intent.'

More angry words and threats followed from the father. He demanded that this attachment must be broken off immediately. Mary replied with floods of tears and sobs most piteous. But farmer Greenacre's heart was unmoved. It was as impervious as stone to all her cries and complaints, her howls of lamentation and her wails of despair.

Farmer Greenacre also had words with the officers of the regiment and as a result soldier William found his duties much increased. For many weeks the young people did not see each other. Christmas came but for William and Mary it was not a time of celebration or festivity. Twelfth Night was empty of any joy or pleasure. The January weather was as bleak and cold as were William and Mary in their blighted expectations and ruined hopes. Then, early in February, a month that was even bleaker and colder than its predecessor, a message came into William's hands. It was from Mary. Could he meet her? She would be waiting for him at the place they had met in happier and warmer times - on the footpath that skirted the southern edge of Hickling Broad at the place called Swim Coots.

But, she warned, he must be punctual because the February weather was so bitter that she could stay for no more than ten minutes after seven o'clock. The tryst was kept. He came to her straight across Hickling Broad. The wind had been from the east for a week and more and it had frozen everything in its path. The surface of the broad was a sheet of ice and this had caused William to fashion a pair of skates.

Together again at last, they embraced and that embrace drove the icy chill from their beings. A few sentences of hastily spoken words and then it was time to part again. Could she return the next night? No. The night after? Yes. He would be waiting. He turned away from her, stepped onto the surface of the broad and soon all she could hear was the swish of his skates.

They met again as they had planned, William gliding across the ice to keep the rendezvous. They arranged another meeting. He would come again in eight days. It would seem an eternity but she could not come sooner. Already farmer Greenacre was getting suspicious. And William had bad tidings too. The threat of French invasion was gone. Napoleon had marched his army to Austria and soon William's regiment would be on the march too. Where? He did not know.

The appointed day arrived. But the weather had changed. The wind had shifted and it no longer had that bite, that cutting edge that went through any body that dared to venture out of doors. It was still cold but no longer was it hunch-up weather.

Mary arrived at the appointed place at the appointed time. But there was no sign of William. Surely he should be there. Where was he? What had happened? A shudder shook Mary from head to toe. She snatched her bonnet from her head. Her hair fell loose and was caught by the wind. She thought she heard something. But what? Could it have been a cry? She held her breath and listened intently. Half a minute later she expelled the air from her lungs in a cloud. She had heard nothing. She waited longer than she should have done. The damp February chill was seeping into her bones. Her own warm breath on her hands was not enough to stop the feeling draining from her fingers and her toes.

She stared out across the broad. There was no movement. There was no sound. Wait! Was that the faint and distant sound of ice creaking and breaking? She saw the moonlight glistening on shallow puddles of water on the surface of the ice. She saw that the ice no longer reached out to grasp the bank. It was at that moment that she knew that she would never see her William again. If he had attempted to skate across to her this night he would have fallen through the ice. And she knew that nothing would have stopped her William from attempting to meet her. But out there in the middle of the broad the ice would have been too thin to support him. Once in the water he would have been beyond all help. Mary turned away and went home, and the next day the regiment marched away.

Occasionally Mary returned to the footpath. Sometimes she would stand and listen. All she wanted to hear just once more was that swish of skates gliding over ice and then feel on her cheek the hot breath of her handsome soldier.

Some people say a phantom skater dressed in the uniform of an English soldier from the time of the Napoleonic wars appears on cold February nights. He skates across the broad and the haunting sound of a martial drumbeat can be heard. Others say the phantom is really that of a young drummer boy. His tale is much the same except that he fell in love while on leave during the winter before the battle of Waterloo.

Potter Heigham is linked to another ghost story but it's certainly a much more incredible tale than the one just related. It goes like this. There was once a rich and eligible bachelor who lived on the other side of the River Thurne in the 18th century.

In the words of Jane Austen, 'It is a truth universally acknowledged, that a single man in possession of a good fortune, must be in want of a wife.' That was the opinion taken by a scheming and ambitious mother. She was determined that he should have a wife and that wife should be her pretty daughter. So she made a pact with an old hag who was skilled in the secret arts, agreeing to pay any price in return for a love potion that was guaranteed to gain the young man's affections. The potion was duly administered, the young man's heart was won and marriage followed. But the mother neglected to pay the witch's price so on the wedding night a coach manned by skeletons pulled up, the terrified bride was snatched from the company and driven off. But when the coach reached the centuries old bridge over the river at Potter Heigham its wheels struck the parapet and coach and horses, skeletons and kidnapped bride all plunged into the river. [There is one place in Broadland where you certainly can see some ghostly skeletons but I'll tell about that in the next chapter.]

A coach driver whose existence in the 18th century is not to be doubted was William Salter who drove the Yarmouth stagecoach for many years. Apparently William met his untimely end at the age of 59 on October 9th 1776 when his team of horses slipped as they were going down the hill beside the church. His epitaph is there for all to see in the wall of Haddiscoe churchyard.

His memorial reads –
Here lies Will Salter, honest man
Deny it Envy if you can
True to his Business & his truft
Always punctual, always just.
His horses cou'd they speak wou'd tell
They lov'd their good old master well.
His up hill work is chiefly done
His Stage is ended. Race is run.
One journey is remaining still,
To climb up Sions holy hill.
And now his faults are all forgiv'n,
Elija like drive up to heaven.
Take the Reward of all his Pains
And leave to other hands the Reins.

I have heard it said that England has more ghosts than any other country. Whatever the truth of it is a good many of the ghost stories involve hard-drinking, hard-riding, and none too pleasant aristocrats and country squires. At Waxham you might well hear the tale of Sir Barney Brograve, a man of short temper and quick fists. He threw a New Year's Eve party for half a dozen of his equally disreputable ancestors whose ghosts appeared by courtesy of the Devil. This gang of knights had all been killed in battle. There was Sir Ralph who was killed in the crusades. Sir Edmund died in the baronial wars of the 13th century and Sir John was one of the few English casualties at Agincourt. Sir Francis got the chop in the Wars of the Roses, Sir Thomas met his end fighting Oliver Cromwell's roundheads, and Sir Charles left this world battling with the French on the field of Ramillies in modern Belgium. The seven of them caroused until midnight at which hour the six had to return to that hot and sulphurous place from whence they came. They say the disreputable seven return each year to continue their boisterous family get-together.

The tale of Brograves and that of the coach crewed by skeletons should not be taken too seriously. But here's a tale about another New Year's Eve party that just might have or could have a tiny core of truth about it. It happened, I was told, in a village where the village church had only one bell back in the 1820s.

A group of seven young men had gathered in the local ale-house determined to see in the New Year as boisterously as the landlord would allow, and as merrily as the somewhat meagre amounts of money in their pockets would permit. They had, however, undertaken to perform one duty at the midnight hour, a duty for which the squire had paid them one shilling in advance. They were to ensure that the church bell was tolled for ten minutes at midnight. They drank and smoked and joked, and the evening hours passed in pleasant merriment and companionship. Eventually the talk turned to the task they had promised to perform. But it was so pleasantly warm in the hostelry and so cold and dark outside that it was soon suggested that surely they need not all go to ring the church bell. After all there was but one bell so therefore only one of their number need go. So who should that one person be?

An old greybeard had sat most of the evening beside the fire, pulling on an old clay pipe and sipping his ale from an old pewter pot. He heard every word. When the young men's voices were raised in friendly dispute the old man stood up, banged his stick across their table and declared, 'Don't none of you go up there tonight. Take my counsel, don't none of you go up there, not this night.'

The young men laughed at his warning.

Why should they not go?

The greybeard smiled. 'Go you up there a bit before or a bit after midnight. I reckon it'd be best if none of you were up there spot on midnight. Leave it a bit either side, that's my counsel.'

The young men pressed him for a reason.

Had they not heard of the white lady? Oh, yes, they had heard that old tale. The white lady, the restless, wandering spirit of a beautiful lady who rose from her grave in search of her one true love. What nonesense! They had never seen her and they'd been around at midnight many a time. The old man smiled and returned to his seat beside the log fire, and the young men resumed their dispute about who should ring the midnight chimes. Eventually, amid much laughter, it was decided. The young man with the loudest voice and the biggest muscles would go, and that was John Gosling.

They drank more and laughed more until Ted Fisher piped up with the words, 'Reckon you'd best be going then, John, bor. Best not keep the white lady waiting.' They all laughed again.

'Huh!' exclaimed muscular John. 'If I see her and she be as beautiful as they say I'll wish her a happy New Year all proper and polite like. Then I'll pick her up in these here arms and give her a great big kiss!' He downed what remained in his tankard, turned on his heel and was gone.

The six remained in the ale-house, downing more of the landlord's best. But gradually the conversation and nervous laughter died away and they all remained silent. Had anyone heard the bell? No. Surely it should have been rung by now. Ted Fisher turned to ask the old man if he had heard the chimes. The old man looked at him and shook his head.

Again they waited in silence. 'I'll wager he's fallen asleep,' said one. 'Aye, he'd had a fair skin full of ale, had he not?' remarked another. 'I'm going up there,' boasted a third and asked, 'Who's coming?'

'We'll all go,' declared Ted. 'No one stays behind this time, come you on!' With that they headed for the door and Ted glanced back toward the fire. There was no old man seated beside the hearth. No stick or pewter pot.

They found John just inside the church door. He was hunched and curled into a ball, his arms pulled tight around his knees and his head was touching the back of his hands. His body was shaking and shivering and from his trembling lips came but three words. 'The white lady,' he whimpered. They were the last words John Gosling ever spoke.

They carried him back to the ale-house but neither ale nor warmth not smelling salts could return him to his senses. Ted Fisher took the landlord aside. 'Where's that old greybeard who was here earlier?' he asked. The landlord stared at him him and shrugged. 'What old greybeard? You lot have been the only ones in here all evening.'

The Victorians liked their tales of unrequited love and they even invented a language of flowers so that young men and women could indicate their emotions without words. No ardent young man would want to receive a daffodil or snowdrop from the object of his desire. They meant regret and consolation. A posy of forget-me-nots indicated true love, and a bouquet of tulips, sweet Williams, strawberries, roses and mignonettes [reseda] sent the message 'Your eyes are beautiful, your smile is perfection, you are forever fair and your qualities surpass your charms.' A sprig of weeping willow sent the message that you were feeling forsaken and marigold indicated jealousy. Honeysuckle was for fidelity, hyacinth was for sorrow, and peach blossom declared 'I am yours!'

These days young men send red roses on St Valentine's Day. But can you guess where and when the first St Valentine's Day message in English was sent? It happened back in February 1477 when Margery Brews, then a girl of about sixteen years, sent a letter to her 'right well beloved valentine.' She wrote, 'I am not in good health of body nor heart, nor shall be till I hear from you.....if you love me, as I trust verily you do, you will not leave me therefore. For, if you had not half the income that you have, and I had to work as hard as any woman alive might do, I would not forsake you. My heart me bids ever more to love you truly over all earthly things.' Margery's mother was all in favour of her daughter's action and a few days earlier she had written to the man who later became her son-in-law reminding him 'Friday is St Valentine's Day when every bird chooses for himself a mate.' Nod, nod, wink, wink. The man the letters were addressed to was John Paston III and he was a member of the Paston family which came originally from the village of that name close to the Norfolk coast. By advantageous marriages and working in the legal profession they rose from yeoman status to become a very wealthy and influential family. They even owned Caister Castle near Great Yarmouth.

In the church at Paston is a brass in memory of Erasmus Paston and his wife Mary. It has a picture of Erasmus and it tells 'Here Erasmus Paston and Mary his wife enclosed are in clay…. of sons three and daughters nine the Lord them parents made ere cruel death did work his cruel spite or fickle life did fade.' It adds that Erasmus died on November 13, 1538.

But why no picture of Mary? And are those words to be believed? It's obvious that Erasmus died first. His picture is there as well as the date of his demise. But there is no likeness of Mary and they did not even put in the date of her death but left the spaces blank so that it reads, 'and Mary his wife deceased ye [space] of [space] .'

At Stokesby there's another example of the date of a wife's death being forgotten or neglected. There the brass states, 'Here lyeth interred ye bodyes of Charles Clere of Stokesby Esq: who dyed ye second day of Novemr Ao 1636 and Elizabeth his wife ye [space] day of [space] Ao Domini 16 [space]'

At Martham there's a memorial stone to a man who, by all accounts, was an upstanding and respected pillar of society back in the days when German George from Hanover became England's King George I. Well, you might say, there's nothing unusual about that. Indeed there is not because many old churches have memorials to respectable members of society who lived long ago, and many of those memorials are little more than eulogies praising those squires, physicians, soldiers, sailors and parsons (and their wives) in the most extravagant and sometimes pompous terms.

But there was none of that in this case. What caused eyebrows to be raised were the words Christopher Burraway used to describe his wife Alice. No, wait a minute, Alice wasn't his wife, she was his sister. No, hang on, she was his mother. What? That can't be right because Alice was his mistress. What is going on?

So there's the puzzle, and it's one that has caused plenty of amusement down the years. If you take it at face value that stone is also a memorial to one almighty scandal. It reads –

Here Lyeth
The Body of Christo
Burraway who Depar
Ted this Life ye 18th day
Of october Anno Domini
1730
Aged 59 years
And their lyes
Alice, who by hir life
Was my sister, my mistress,
My mother and my wife.
Dyed Feb ye 12 1729
Aged 76 years.

There's a roughly carved hand with a finger pointing to the right at the end of the line 'And their lyes'. How could a woman be one man's sister, mistress, mother and wife? That's a scandal indeed! So a scurrilous story was constructed to give meaning to the conundrum and titillate the imaginations of those who looked upon it. That story went something like this. Alice Burraway and her farmer father were very close. In fact they were a little too close on at least one occasion because in 1672 Alice gave birth to a baby boy. The child was brought up in an orphanage until it was time for him to make his way in the world. Ignorant of his parentage, he turned up in Martham looking for a job. Christopher's father-grandfather had died and the farm was Alice's and she had need of a strong and energetic young man to shoulder the agricultural duties. Christopher was taken on and he proved more than competent and together they prospered.

The years passed and an affectionate bond developed between them and the twenty-year difference in their ages was dismissed as being of no importance. They decided to marry and marry they did. Here the story takes something of an incredible twist. One day, after two decades of married life, Alice noticed a distinctive birthmark on her husband's shoulder. Horror! She remembered that the child of whom she had been delivered many years before had had a birthmark just like it.

For Alice it was a tremendous shock and the more she thought about it the more dreadful it became. She questioned Christopher and he confirmed that indeed he had been raised as an orphan. The pieces fell into place. The terrible revelation was true! The knowledge that she had married her own son was too much for Alice and she died aged 76. Christopher's world was shattered and some 18 months later he followed the woman who was his sister, mistress, mother and wife to the grave.

Now for the explanation. There was nothing unusual about Christopher Burraway's birth. Like hundreds of other first-born sons in those days he took his father's name. Unfortunately Christopher Burraway senior died not many months after his son's birth. Life wasn't easy for a widow with a young child so a few months later Christopher's mother, still a young woman, married again taking as her second husband one Gregory Johnson. They soon had two children – a boy and a girl - before cruel death intervened again. Christopher's mother went to an early grave leaving Gregory three young children to care for. As was usual in those days, Gregory quickly found himself another wife. Her name was Alice and she was a widow with a son of her own to care for. At about the turn of the century Gregory Johnson died and two years later Christopher aged 30 married Alice, his late stepfather's widow who was getting on for 50. Christopher was a respectable and respected member of the community, and he took on what was then an important and powerful position in society, the post of a churchwarden.

No doubt Christopher looked upon Alice much like a sister when she, a young woman, married his stepfather. She was his mistress in the sense that when he was young she had parental authority over him and she was certainly his legal wife for getting on for three decades. The memorial stone with its enigmatic words shows that Christopher Burraway was a man who was loyal and devoted to his wife, and he was a man with a great sense of humour too.

Now for a tale about a young woman whose total lack of fear of spooks and spectres resulted in her making a most advantageous and happy marriage. Mary was pretty enough to turn the heads of most young men, but she was not one of those delicate blooms for whom a comfortable marriage was the only ambition. Mary had personality and character in abundance.

The problem for Mary was that her father liked beer more than was good for either his pocket or his health. He was always inviting friends round to join him in the business of downing more than a few pints. Then they would munch their way through puddings and pies before setting about the business of downing yet more pints.

It happened one January night when the cold fingers of an east wind were seeking entry through every crack and crevice of the cottage. The draughts nipped at the toes and ears of Mary's marshman father and his friends. And what made it worse for them was that when they called on Mary to recharge their tankards with good strong beer she called back that they had drunk it all and the barrel was emptier than a beggar's purse. 'Then get you on down to the beer house,' shouted her father, tossing a couple of coins at her.

'She'll never do it!' exclaimed his friend the blacksmith. It was a statement the butcher, the baker and the candlestick-maker noisily endorsed. 'That's too dark outside for a chit of girl like your Mary,' declared the butcher. 'Aye, it's far too cold and dark out there for a mawther like Mary,' declared the baker. 'She'll freeze to death if she ain't spooked to death first,' declared the candlestick-maker with a laugh.

'Huh!' retorted the farmer. 'She may be but a chit of a girl but she's not afraid of nothing in this world, and that's a fact.' Mary turned on her heel, pulled a shawl over her head and left the room. Twenty minutes later she was back with two jugs of foaming ale, enough to ensure that the five men slept like logs and snored like hogs right through what remained of that night.

The next morning all five men had thick heads and little recollection of what had passed during the previous evening. But they did remember how Mary had stepped out into the darkness without so much as a word of complaint or apprehension. The blacksmith stood up and, after making sure that Mary was not within earshot, issued a challenge to his marshman friend. He would set Mary a task that she would never dare to undertake.

'How much will you wager?' said the marshman.

'Name the sum, and treble it for us,' was the chorus reply from the butcher, the baker and the candlestick-maker.

'Ten guineas a man! Or is that too rich for your liking?' retorted the marshman.

'Done!' bellowed the blacksmith.

'Done!' retorted Mary's father, spitting on the palm of his hand and offering it to each of the four in turn. 'Done! Come you all back in a week and state your challenge. And be sure you've got them ten golden guineas apiece!'

Two days later, on Monday, the blacksmith and his three friends sneaked into the snug of the village beer house and over their pint pots they talked in hushed and conspiratorial tones. After half an hour they were joined by an old man whose well-worn coat and breeches were almost as thin and shiny as the skin of his bald pate. Immediately their noses began to twitch and wriggle. Wave upon wave of the foulest stench imaginable wafted over them from the old man's body, from his clothes and from his cavernous and toothless mouth. The smell was worse than that of any neglected privy or cart that collected the night soil.

'No, I'll not do it. Not for a shilling I won't,' grunted the old man.

'Will you for two?' asked the baker, pinching his nose.

'No. Nor for three shillings neither. But make it a crown and I'm your man.'

'Done, master sexton,' said the blacksmith. 'You know what's to be done. There's to be no mistakes. Just scare her good and proper. That's all you've got to do. Here's three shillings. There'll be two more when the job's done.'

The malodorous sexton departed and the four friends jumped up and waved their broad brimmed hats in an effort to scatter the stinking cloud he had bequeathed to them.

The next Saturday the four made their way to the marshman's cottage which stood up the narrow lane beyond the churchyard.

'So what's your challenge for my fearless girl?' was the greeting.

'She's got to go to the church when the clock strikes the

midnight hour. Then she's got to go down into the crypt - here's the key - to where they got all them old bones piled up and she's got to bring us back the biggest skull she can find.'

'Is that all? She'll not turn a hair at that!' declared the marshman.

'Maybe not, but I reckon what hair she's got left will be turned white when she gets back,' chuckled the candlestick-maker.

The five men drank and played their games of dice and cards, and drank some more. They heard the clock chime the half-hour after eleven and their chatter and laughter subsided when they heard the up-quarter strike. Another five minutes passed and the marshman spoke. 'I reckon 'tis nigh on time,' he said. The others nodded and Mary was called in from the kitchen and given her instructions. She was to go to the church and bring back the biggest skull from among the pile of bones in the crypt. Without a word she picked up the big key, wrapped her shawl over her head and departed.

Once inside the big squeaking church door, she lit her candle, unlocked the door that led down to the charnel room and descended. She reached out for the nearest skull.

'Don't you touch that!' moaned the sexton in a slow and sonorous voice.

Mary's hand moved toward another white and shiny skull bone.

'Don't you touch me neither!' the sexton intoned.

'Hold your peace!' snapped Mary. 'I'll take whichever I choose.' With that she picked up two skulls, weighed them in her hands, gave a sigh of satisfaction and with candle in one hand and a skull in the other she turned and ascended the stairs. The perplexed sexton gave voice to a string of mournful moans such as he thought would scare anyone. Then, to his great dismay, he heard the key turn in the door at the top of the stairs.

Not ten minutes later Mary marched into the kitchen where the five were gathered. She unwrapped the skull from her shawl and banged it down in the table along with the big iron key. The jaws of the blacksmith, the butcher, the baker and the candlestick-maker all dropped.

'That'll be ten guineas apiece, if you please,' chortled the marshman.

The four conspirators went home in silence and when the morning light was bright and clear they released the foul-smelling sexton from his dungeon.

Soon the story of fearless Mary's midnight adventure was the talk of the parish. A day later it was the talk of five parishes more. One day more and it came to the ears of the young squire who was the marshman's landlord. He lived alone in a rambling old manor house where the floorboards creaked and the windows rattled. And he lived alone because no servant or cook or maid would stay in the house because of the ghost, the ghost of his mother who had died getting on for two years previously.

The young man mounted his horse and rode as swiftly as he could to the marshman's cottage. He offered to cancel the rent if Mary would come to work at the manor. The deal was done and Mary packed a bag, wrapped the shawl around her head and shoulders and mounted the horse behind the squire.

He explained that his mother's restless ghost made life in the big house almost intolerable. She had been an oppressive disciplinarian in life and she remained so in death. She moved things. She opened doors and windows. She snatched things from people's hands, even from their lips at dinner. Was it any wonder that he lived alone?

For the first few days Mary worked hard in an effort to restore a semblance of domestic order. She cooked and cleaned, and she watched and noted everything that happened. On the fifth night she served the meal having carefully laid a third place at the table.

During the meal she conversed eagerly with the squire, but for as much as she spoke with him she would turn and speak most pleasantly to the invisible person who apparently occupied the third place. The days became weeks and Mary continued to have conversations with the invisible person. She taught the squire to do the same when he felt his mother's presence. Life settled down. No longer were doors slammed or chairs turned upside down or pots and pans thrown across the kitchen.

One day when the sky was bright and cloudless, Mary was at her chores as usual when she again felt a presence in the room. She turned and saw the shimmering figure of an old woman approaching. She wiped her hands on her apron and said gaily, 'It is a fine morning, is it not, my lady?'

The spectre halted and indicated to Mary that she should follow. 'Lead you on, ma'am,' she said firmly. 'I have no fear of you.'

The ghost led Mary down into the old, cobwebbed and musty-smelling cellars. Mary paused to reach for a candle. 'You have no need of that, or are you afraid of the darkness?' said a woman's voice.

'No, I'm not. Lead you on. But I'll bring this candle. No dead old woman is going to tell me what to do while I live and breathe!' said Mary, her tone determined and resolute.

Mary felt the damp air suddenly begin to stir. The candle flame swayed and flickered. Then the movement in the air was stilled and the flame stood bright and steady again. There was dust everywhere, and so thick was it that it muffled her footsteps. Eventually the ghost halted, pointed a finger at a corner of the wall and said, 'There! Look there, daring and dauntless girl.'

Mary obeyed. Some of the bricks were loose and were easily moved. Mary reached in and her fingers closed around two drawstring purses.

A week passed and the ghost of the squire's mother made not a single appearance. After two weeks the young squire asked Mary if she had seen the spectre or felt its presence. 'No,' she replied, 'not for a good fortnight. 'Tis my opinion we'll not see her again.'

Her words proved to be true. Things remained quiet and well ordered, and one evening Mary arrived at the dinner table wearing a new gown of silk and a necklace of pearls. 'Where did you....' began the squire. Mary motioned him to be silent and placed a silver platter in front of him. On it were two new drawstring purses which she raised in turn and shook close to his ears so that he could hear the heart-warming sound of coins of gold jingling against yet more coins of gold. He smiled in delight and stared at the purses of soft white leather, one as large as a quart jug and the other half as much again. He reached forward and his hand hovered over the larger one.

'That one's mine,' said Mary.

'Yours?' replied the squire.

'Yes, mine. The smaller one is yours.'

'I'll wager you found them both in this house, therefore both are mine.'

'I found them here, that's true. And you have the strength to take them from me. But if you do you must also take back a ghost and a lonely life lived in an empty house'

The squire fell silent and moved his hand over the smaller of the two purses and lifted it to feel its weight. 'You could have the larger one too, for a price,' said Mary softly.

'What price?' queried the young squire.

'Naught but a gold ring for my marriage finger and the

proper fee for the parson when he makes us man and wife.'

The squire pushed his chair back from the table and looked hard at Mary.

'So, what is your answer?' she whispered.

He did not speak. There was no need for him to speak because his smile spoke all the words that were necessary.

The squire and the daring girl lived happily together for the rest of their days. Light and laughter returned to the old manor house from which all dust and cobwebs were banished. The marshman continued to drink and play at dice and cards with his friends the blacksmith, the butcher, the baker and the candlestick-maker. Once a month Mary visited her father's small cottage up the lane past the church and on one of those days in high summer the five challenged her once more. She smiled at them and went home to the manor.

But when they all went to church the next Sunday they did not have to screw up their noses or pinch their nostrils. The sexton had been scrubbed as clean as a doorstep on a Monday, and his coat and hose and shoes were as new as a bright new pin. Some of the congregation even declared that they suspected that he had rubbed lavender water into his shining bald pate.

P.S.

Question, who was it who first said that the course of true love never did run smooth?

Answer, William Shakespeare, 'A Midsummer Night's Dream' act 1, scene 1, line 135.

Ghosts, Giants, Dragons and Angels

There's a very old building in a lonely little place on the edge of the Halvergate Marshes where you can see three ghosts at any time. You don't have to spend hours waiting around hoping they might appear. They are there all the time. They are three skeletons that have just got up out of their graves.

They are painted on one wall of Wickhampton church and they are part of a huge picture that was painted long ago with the intention of reminding you and me of our mortality. The Black Death in the mid-1300s was a huge shock to the social and religious system and many people interpreted it as God's judgement for the sins of society. One result was that a macabre and morbid fascination with death developed and the story involving those three skeletons became very popular. The tale of the three living and the three dead was a story from earlier times but the Church gleefully adopted it as a warning to people to be ready for death and judgement.

It was a story about three young kings in the prime of life who spent their time enjoying all the worldly pleasures of the day. They are usually depicted out hunting, dressed in their finery and without a care in the world. Accompanied by their servants and hunting dogs, they venture deeper and deeper into the forest until they are suddenly confronted by three gruesome corpses. These spirits of the dead rise up in front of them to warn them that inevitably they must die too - 'as ye are so once were we, as we are now so shall ye be'. It is a phrase that has been repeated on many tombstones and memorials across the land.

In the same church are the effigies of a smiling knight and his rather more grim-faced lady. The knight has his sword and shield and he wears state-of-the-art military armour of the late 13th century. She wears a wimple and a long flowing robe, the high fashion for ladies of the same period. They date from around the time when King Edward I was building his castles in Wales to hold down that conquered country while fighting new wars in Scotland.

The knight is Sir William Gerbrygge and he holds a heart in his hands. It is thought that his lady once held a heart in her hands too and that gave rise to a tale about two brothers named Hampton who owned adjoining estates and got into a long and bitter quarrel about where the boundary should be. Eventually they came to blows and the struggle was so fierce that they ended up tearing the hearts out of one another. God was so angry by this terrible fratricidal conflict that the two bodies were turned to stone as warnings against such behaviour. They were placed in Wickhampton church for all to see and there they remain. And another result was that one place was called Wickhampton – shortened from Wicked Hampton – and the other place was called Hell Fire Gate, now reduced to Halvergate.

There are stone effigies of two more knights in armour in Ingham church. There is a local tale that says that once a year they rise from their tombs to fight a foreign enemy. They are Sir Oliver de Ingham who died in 1344 and Sir Roger de Bois.

It was an old belief that the people most likely to see a ghost were those called 'chime children'. They were people who had been born at the chime hours of the night – nine o'clock in the evening, midnight, and three and six o'clock in the morning. And Hallowe'en was considered the 'liveliest' night of the year for the appearance of these wailing apparitions. It was the night when, according to one writer who lived several hundred years ago, 'all dead souls, witches, warlocks and fairies have leave to wander the world as they desire, and men are wiser to stay within their houses with the doors barred and the windows shuttered'. Another group of people likely to see ghosts were those who were themselves close to death.

It was suggested that you should grow houseleek [sempervivum] on the roof of your house because 'it banishes ghosts and keeps the house safe from thunder, lightning, the evil eye, all pestilence and bad witchery'. If you suspected that your house was haunted by invisible spirits and you wanted to be able to see them it was suggested that you should 'secure the brain of a cock, dust enough taken from a coffin to fill a silver thimble, oil of crushed almonds and walnuts and some virgin wax; mix it all well and fashion in the likeness of a bird'. Then you should 'sleep with this under your pillow for three nights and on the next day at your rising you shall see, if you fear nothing, the spirits that inhabit the air and also many wonders and marvels.' The houseleek was a remarkable plant because one famous apothecary said that its juice was good for fluxes in the bowels, fretting ulcers, cankers, tetters, ringworms, gout, warts and corns, easing the 'distempered heat of the brain' and by putting its leaves on your head you could stop nose bleeds.

Sometimes people believe they have witnessed ghostly activity when in fact they have let their imaginations run away with them or someone has played a trick on them. I was told of a couple of newly-weds whose honeymoon near Filby came to a frightening conclusion. At least that's what they thought until the cold light of day revealed what had really happened. There had been a thunderstorm during the previous evening but eventually the thunder and lightning had moved away leaving a steady rain falling. During the night the couple were awakened by a soft but regular tapping noise overhead. Then the noise would stop for several minutes before starting again and seeming to be considerably louder.

They stared up at the ceiling not knowing what to do. Eventually the young wife prevailed upon her husband to investigate. He groped his way to the light switch. Over the bed there was a sudden flash and the room was filled with a nasty smell of burning. The young man dived back under the covers and overhead the steady and regular noise returned. The new day dawned bright and clear and revealed what had happened. The rain had found its way in and had dripped down onto the ceiling above their heads and had then followed the light cable. When the young man had switched on the light there was a flash and the smell of burnt rubber cable.

Back in the days before sewers and mains drainage it was what country folk called the honeywagon or honeycart that came round to collect the nightsoil – that's the very smelly and rather unpleasant stuff that accumulated in privies and chamber pots. There was never any doubt about the location of the honeywagon. One summer evening when the air was still and the honeywagon 'perfume' was remarkably pungent, three holidaying townies were staggering up the road on their way home from the local hostelry where they had imbibed most plentifully. They noticed the honeywagon standing in the road. They got aboard and coaxed the horse into a trot. Unfortunately for them the tank had not been sealed and soon the contents were sloshing around until eventually they overflowed. The three young men had plenty of time to regret their prank as they trudged back to their rented lodging with a most unenticing aroma soaked deep into their hair and clothes.

Over the centuries pranksters have played many trick on newlyweds on their wedding nights. In the old days it was the custom for the couple and their guests to drink the sack-posset [a mixture of milk, wine, egg yolks, sugar, cinnamon and nutmeg] and eat pieces of the wedding cake. Those who were single had to have a bite or two of the cake because it was believed that they would then dream of their intended mate. The last act was to see the happy couple tucked up in their bed and then fling the stocking. The newlyweds would sit up in bed in their nightshirts and the unmarried guests would take it in turns to sit at the foot of the bed and throw the bride's and groom's stockings backwards over their heads. If a young lady managed to get the stocking to land on the groom's head it was a sign that she too would soon be married. Then at last the couple would be left alone. But it was not always the end of the 'waggery' and pranks, and the young men would often try to give the newlyweds a scary experience. Fiendish wails and hoots would be accompanied by knockings and scratchings and caterwauling at the door and windows. One trick was to attach walnut-shells to the paws of a cat and loose the unfortunate feline in the roof space where it would gallop noisily back and forth over the heads of the distracted couple.

Back in the 18th century at Ranworth there lived a hard-drinking, hard-riding and hard-swearing squire who would, no doubt, have approved of such boisterous behaviour. One of his vices – and he had many – was his willingness to take a bet on just about anything. But while he was only too willing to take a bet, he was not very keen to paying up when he lost and he lost more times than he won. His debts piled up secured against his home and estate. Then one day he challenged a rival to a horserace from Ranworth to Wroxham and the purse for the winner would have been more than enough to clear the debts. The match was set for a bright and crisp New Year's Eve morning. At first the two stayed together as they cantered across the frosty countryside. But as they galloped along the edge of Salhouse Broad the squire's rival began to inch ahead. The Ranworth squire spurred his horse into one last effort and when he was level he pulled out a pistol from his saddle holster and fired. The shot killed his opponent's horse instantly but also had the consequence of killing his rival in the fall. That night as the squire celebrated the approach of another year, the spectre of his dead rival appeared at midnight and carried the squire away to his deserved punishment. It is said that the squire's final minutes are re-enacted at midnight each New Year's Eve.

Maybe the sinful squire of Ranworth purchased his drinking spirits from the gangs of smugglers who ran contraband from Holland and France into England across the flat beaches of the East Coast. They say that the keepers of the drainage windmills of Broadland colluded with the smugglers by setting the sails in a certain position to give warning when revenue men were in the district. Most of the drainage mills that remain in Broadland were built in the 19th century and the tallest is Berney Arms mill built about 1865.

Later some of the drainage mills were powered by steam and petrol engines before the installation of electricity powered pumps brought an end to reliance on wind power. The old drainage mills are one of Broadland's most picturesque features and artists and photographers have recorded their images in all seasons. I heard of two visitors who were very surprised when they compared the results of their efforts. They had each taken several shots of an old mill near Stalham, one using a digital camera and one using film. They had taken their pictures at the same time so they were more than a little surprised to see that while they both had pleasing pictures of the mill, one set of prints clearly showed the figure of a woman in old fashioned dress standing outside the mill and looking rather irately in their direction.

The drainage mills of Broadland are an eye-catching and

distinctive feature of the landscape and they have been likened to giants marching across the flat marshlands. Now they are being joined by a new generation of 'giants' - the tall white turbines designed to harness the energy of the wind. Among the first to be built were those at West Somerton, and that is perhaps as it should be because in the churchyard of the village church are deposited 'the mortal remains of Robert Hales the Norfolk giant whose height was 7 feet 8 inches'. In his prime Robert stood 2.34 metres tall, weighed some 33 stones and had a 64-inch [1.62 metre] chest. Born in 1813, Robert came from a family of six-footers, and he had a sister more than seven feet tall. Robert found it difficult to gain ordinary employment and inevitably was drawn into show business touring Britain and America. He died in 1865. No doubt Robert was familiar with the much older 'giant' in the church, the wall painting of St Christopher whose story was told on page 84.

Not far from Great Yarmouth are the remains of a castle that was built by a man who had something of a giant reputation in his day. He was Sir John Fastolf who is said by some to have been the inspiration for Will Shakespeare's Falstaff. Sir John made his fortune in the wars against France in the early 15th century. Indeed much of the cash to pay for the building of the castle at Caister came from his foreign escapades which included receiving hefty ransoms for aristocratic French prisoners. And by one of those coincidences that crops up in history, one of Sir John's most memorable victories was that against the odds in what came to be called the Battle of the Herrings deep in France. One wonders if the herrings involved came from his birthplace of Yarmouth.

Sir John was in command of a convoy of 300 wagons taking supplies to the troops fighting in the siege of Orleans.

It was February 1429, and on the wagons were lots of barrels of salted herrings. A force of 3,000 French and Scots intercepted the convoy but they were chased off by Sir John and his 1,000 English archers. Sir John died in 1459 and was buried at St Benet's Abbey.

The castle, one of the first to be built of bricks in England, then passed to the Paston family but they had trouble keeping hold of it. In 1469 John Mowbray, Duke of Norfolk, decided he wanted the castle for himself and he attacked with an army several hundreds strong. Inside the castle was the widow Lady Margaret Paston, some of her children, and two dozen retainers who were lacking in victuals, gunpowder and arrows. It was a blockade more than active siege although the defenders killed two men when they fired off a cannon. Eventually the Pastons surrendered but they got their castle back a few years later. A century later the family built themselves newer and more comfortable accommodation beside the River Bure at Oxnead and some of the cash for that came from another martial exploit. There in the church is a memorial to Clement Paston who, like Sir John Fastolf, made a financial killing when he captured a French admiral and kept him prisoner at Caister until a handsome ransom was handed over.

There is another castle not far from Great Yarmouth that is a lot older than Sir John Fastolf's castle at Caister. In fact it is a thousand years older and dates from the time when this part of the world was ruled by emperors in Rome. The walls of the Roman fort at Burgh Castle are made of flint and brick and are almost 3 metres thick and rise to more than 4 metres high in places. It's a haunting and, so I have been told, a haunted place.

After the end of Roman rule the local Anglo-Saxon king gave the old fort to some wandering Irish monks and they

used it as their monastery. War with another king made the
monks move on and when the Normans came they used the
old walls as the outer defence of a motte and bailey castle. So
it is not surprising that there have been reports of people
seeing spectral Roman soldiers and Viking warriors while
others have said that they have heard the noise of ancient
battles being fought again.

Down river from Oxnead, between Coltishall and
Wroxham, the River Bure makes a large U-turn and high on
the left bank is the church at Belaugh. There a 'godly trooper'
from the age of Cromwell's war against King Charles
scratched out the faces of the painted saints.

Half a century later, so the story goes, a servant at the
rectory stole plate and cash and buried it in the garden. A few
days later he returned to dig up his ill-gotten gains.
Unfortunately for him, he was seen making off with a sack
thrown over his shoulder and a chase ensued. He tried to
escape by swimming across the river but his sack was too
heavy and he drowned. On calm nights, so they say, the
phantom of that thief is sometimes to be seen rising to the
surface of the water before being dragged under again by the
weight of his loot.

There is a tale that the famous screen paintings in
Ranworth church were the work of an artistic monk from
nearby St Benet's Abbey and that his troubled ghost still
makes the journey between the church and ruined monastery.
It's a tale which, like many others that seem to date from the
1920s and 1930s, has been retold and recycled many times in
books and magazines, as have those stories of the nasty squire
who was whisked away on New Year's Eve, the phantom
wherry, and the crashing coach at Potter Heigham's old
bridge. But I had not heard the strange tale of the brothers
Isaac and Uriah Rope until I was told it over a pint in The

Maltsters at Ranworth which was called the Jolly Farmers back in Victorian times. I must caution you that my informant had a twinkle in her eye and a smile on her lips as she related it, but there are elements within the tale that hint that it might not all be 'a load of squit' as they say in Norfolk.

Back in the 18th century two brothers worked together on their farm. They were big strong men and Isaac was the elder by a couple of years. But in most other respects they were as alike as two peas in a pod – they dressed alike, they talked alike, they thought alike and they looked very much alike but for the colour of their hair, Isaac's being a darker hue of brown. They were an industrious but unadventurous pair, and so self-sufficient were they that they rarely had reason to leave the farm. Then, one day in early summer, they did have cause leave. That cause was the wedding of a distant cousin and at the celebration they saw a pretty young woman by the name of Sarah Rook. Instantly the brothers were smitten though they did not say anything to each other or to pretty Sarah.

Back on the farm the brothers attempted to settle back into their routine but they each detected that something was wrong. They were both off their food; they were increasingly forgetful of their chores; and they both seemed to live in a daze. Both of them were well and truly lovesick. They both suspected the problem and their suspicions grew stronger when each started to invent reasons for leaving the farm more often than they had ever done before. And worse, Uriah began to shave every day and spend money at a rate that became a bone of contention. And so the truth came out and after a long and heated debate it was decided that the only solution was to arrange a face-to-face meeting with Miss Rook at which each would confess his admiration of her, and then she would be asked to decide their destinies.

Miss Rook obliged and a meeting was duly held attended by the two brothers, the attractive object of their desires, and for the sake of propriety, an elderly aunt who was conveniently somewhat hard of hearing and who remained discreetly seated in a far corner of the room.

Unfortunately for Uriah his fashionable new waistcoat, the aroma of his lavender water and his precisely combed hair exacted no comment from the pretty young miss who displayed an obvious partiality for Isaac. Uriah watched in silence as his brother and Sarah engaged in warm conversation and exchanged glances charged with a meaning that he could not fail to detect. After ten minutes he made a noisy and petulant exit and made his way to the nearest alehouse where he sought to drown the painful musings of rejection that whirled within his brain.

The next day he called again on Sarah and noisily announced that his affection for her exceeded by far that of his brother, and that if she refused his proposal of marriage he had no desire to live. He declared most vehemently that he was determined to kill himself within ten minutes of any rejection. What was her answer to be? Poor Sarah, what was she to do? Sorrow and unhappiness awaited one, two, or perhaps all three of them whichever course she took. She looked at Uriah and the passion and misery that she believed she saw in his eyes convinced her that he would carry out his deadly threat. She determined that she could never allow herself to be the cause of such a fatal conclusion, even at the cost of her own joy.

Isaac accepted the melancholy destruction of his hopes without one word of anger or dispute, but on the eve of the wedding day he packed a bag and departed the house that had been his home since the day of his birth. Sarah and Uriah were married and soon Uriah's protestations of eternal love and kindness were but memories. He spent more and more of the little money that they had on drink, and fewer and fewer of his sober hours at work on the farm. Fortunately Sarah proved to be a strong and resilient spirit and week after week, month after month, she toiled from dawn to dusk in the forlorn hope that one day life would get better. Certainly things could not get worse.

Seven years passed and Sarah's anguish, disillusion, and the endless round of toil gradually and most cruelly eroded her enchanting grace and her fair and flawless form. In the cold midwinter her spirit buckled and her weary body refused to tolerate further the demands of crushing labour. Pain and disease invaded her being. Hope, thin as it was, gave way to grim despair and life itself became a cheerless and oppressive burden.

Then, one evening at the end of harvest when the soft light of twilight was fading fast and when Sarah had been forced to take to her bed, she heard voices raised in dispute. Slowly she descended the stairs. She almost fainted at the sight that she beheld. Her husband Uriah was slumped in his chair as usual, a bottle in one hand, a tankard in the other. And standing in front of him and glaring down at him with eyes filled with contempt was Isaac.

Uriah turned his head and saw Sarah enter the room. He laughed scornfully and yelled at Isaac, 'Take her, brother! You can have her! I don't want her! I'll sell her to you for five guineas and a bottle of rum. What say you?'

'I'll not buy my brother's wife!' shouted Isaac. 'But I tell you this, brother mine, she shall not stay here with you one moment longer.' He pointed at Sarah and yelled again. 'Can you not see what you and your ways have done to her?'

Uriah laughed again, rose from his chair and aimed a blow with the bottle at Isaac's head. Isaac ducked, Sarah screamed and Uriah tumbled to the floor. Drunkenly he staggered to his feet, turned his back on them, kicked open the door and disappeared into the darkening night. Sarah collapsed onto a chair, her cries and sobs punctuating the lengthening bouts of rasping coughs.

'Fetch him back, Isaac. Fetch him back, please,' she said in a soft voice. 'God knows I hate him, but I shall not have him come to harm on my account.'

Outside rain had begun to fall and soon the well-worn path from the house was transformed into a slippery muddy track. Isaac heard his brother's shouts ahead and ran and slid after him. The cold rain ran down his face and soaked into his clothes. Then he heard Uriah's shouts off to the right. He was going toward the river and the broad!

When he found Uriah his arms were flailing as he desperately attempted to gain a firm hold on something. But the black mud was sucking him back. For a few moments Isaac stood over him, unable or unwilling to decide if he should stretch out a life-saving hand. Uriah was sliding backwards, deeper and deeper into the mud, all his efforts at self-preservation overcome by exhaustion. Isaac felt someone brush past him. It was Sarah. She fell to her knees and reached out. Uriah grabbed at her hand and clasped it tight. But still he sank deeper. Isaac yelled at him to release Sarah. Uriah spat mud from his mouth and yelled, 'She's my wife! Mine! Not yours!'

Isaac grabbed at Sarah but her thin muddied body slipped through his hold. Not one of them uttered a further cry or curse. The rain came on. The tragedy was complete.

For seven more years Isaac lived alone in the house where he was born. Each night, an hour before sunset he walked the path to the river and the broad, and there he stood in silence until darkness filled the sky. They say he wanted to hear

Sarah's soft voice once more and feel her hand touch his. For exactly seven years without interruption he adhered to that lonely ritual. Then he vanished too. Some said he went back to sea. Some said he went abroad to fight in a foreign war. Some said there were other explanations.

That was the story I was told. And as I said earlier there was a glint in my informant's eye when she related the tale.

'So what do you think happened?' I asked.

'How should I know what happened?' she said with a smile. 'But I'll tell you this, I know someone who swears she's seen the ghosts of a pretty little woman and two big men down by the broad on a fine September night.'

'Who saw them?' I asked.

'Someone who at this very moment is not a million miles from here,' she replied. 'Another white wine if you please, kind sir.'

You can see the stone and rather ghostly image a young woman of graceful modesty and excellent virtue whose early death left her husband distraught in Rollesby church. She is Rose Claxton who died childless in 1601. She lies rather uncomfortably on her right side with her head on the palm of one hand. She wears the ruff collar, tight bodice and farthingale that were fashionable in the days of Shakespeare and Guy Fawkes. Rose died at the age of 23 after just seven years of marriage. She was buried 'with the excessive tears of her friends, especially of her sorrowful husband who has made his heart a treasury of her excellent virtue and this sepulchre one monument of his perpetual love.' Some 250 years later a memorial was put up on the wall to a reverend gentleman who served the parish for forty years, and his wife. It also served as a 'sad memorial of sorrows caused by the premature loss of seven of their children'. Another fifty years passed at Rollesby and tragedy visited the village again and they put up a memorial in the churchyard to several young men who drowned while fishing on Rollesby Broad.

Indeed, the land of the Broads has seen many tragic events. One of the worst was when the Ferry Inn at Horning was destroyed by German bombs in 1941 with the deaths of more than 20 people. The inn was rebuilt in the 1960s and there is a tale that the ghost of a young woman abused by naughty monks from St Benet's sometimes puts in an appearance.

Certainly there are places you can go to in Broadland to escape the hustle and bustle of modern life. Indeed, if you really want to get away from it all you can go to 'Nowhere'. True, it's not a joke. That's what they called a marshy area near Acle that was added to the parish in the 1800s. There's a story that a local lad was making his rather erratic way home from a pub one night when he was stopped by a constable. 'Hello, hello, and where do you think you're going?' said the bobby.

'Nowhere,' was the reply.

'Is that so? And where are you from?'

'Nowhere.'

'I see. You come from nowhere and you're going nowhere,' said the constable with some sarcasm in his voice.

'Yes, Nowhere near Acle!' All was resolved.

Oh, yes! What about dragons and angels? It is recorded that a dragon made its home at Ludham many years ago. It would come out at night to terrorise the district. So one brave soul volunteered to ring the church bell when the beast was on the prowl. That made the dragon very angry and it started to come out during the day as well. One day, while it was out of the way, a resourceful villager rammed a big stone into the mouth of the dragon's lair. When the beast returned it tried in vain to remove the obstruction. Angrily the creature stalked off to the ruins of St Benet's Abbey where it buried itself in the cellars and was never seen again.

As for angels you won't see any more beautiful than those painted on the screen at Barton Turf church. There are the nine orders along with St Apollonia who helps with toothache. There's also St Barbara the protectress against lightening and cannonballs which made her the patron saint of artillerymen, and St Citha who was invoked by wives when they lost their keys and by travellers when crossing rivers. And there are four kings too. There's the murdered King Henry VI, and King Olaf of Norway with two loaves of bread to identify him. Poor Olaf came to a violent end but achieved popularity in medieval England and gave his name to St Olaves where they built a priory in his honour beside the River Waveney. And the last two are kings who, a long time ago, were patron saints of England – St Edward the Confessor and St Edmund. St Edmund with his arrows, yes, that's where we began.

So are there such things as ghosts? Well, there are plenty of sceptics. 'Don't let us make imaginary evils when you know we have so many real ones to encounter,' declared Oliver Goldsmith.

Doctor Johnson declared, 'It is wonderful that five thousand years have elapsed since the creation of the world, and still it is undecided whether or not there has ever been an instance of the spirit of any person appearing after death. All argument is against it; but all belief is for it.'

Let's leave the last word to Shakespeare's Hamlet. He saw the ghost of his father and declared, 'There are more things in heaven and earth, Horatio, than are dreamt of in your philosophy.'

Doing things diff'rent

As many visitors have found out people tend to do things a bit different in Broadland and rural East Anglia than they do in other parts of the kingdom. And out in the most rural parts you can still come across a way with words that might have you scratching your head and wondering if English is the native tongue .

Here are some words that have been used in the past – and some still are. A harnser is a heron; hodmadod or dodman means a snail; hulver is holly; a kittling is a young cat; mingins are gnats; a bandy or sukey is a hare; a carr is a small clump of trees usually by a river; burbles are small pimples such as those caused by the stinging of nettles or insect bites.

A betsy was a kettle; a quant is a boat pole, mawkin means a scarecrow; a loke is a blind alley or narrow lane; a score is a path down to the riverside; staithe means quay or landing stage; the rows are narrow passageways in old parts of Yarmouth; yelm is a bundle of reeds or straw for use in thatching; a tittermatorter is a see-saw; a shiver is a splinter; a snack is a door latch; a dwile is a floor cloth; hunch-weather is cold weather that makes you hunch up your shoulders.

Bor is used as 'you' when addressing a man or boy; mawther means a young woman, sometimes used as female equivalent of bor; ruffatory was a rude and boisterous boy fond of horse-play, described in one old book as a lad who often comes home 'with a bloody nose, a bump upon his head, or with his clothes half torn off, or dirty from being rolled in the mire'. According to an old book of Norfolk dialect words a fangast was a marriageable maid, and 'to give a girl a green gown' was a phrase used to describe romping with a girl in the grass so that her dress was stained green in activity that went beyond the bounds of innocent amusement.

A lummox is an awkward or clumsy person; lug means ear so to get a ding on the ear was to get a clip round the ear; smittick is a very small portion; squit means nonsense; titty-totty means very small. To dringle is to waste time in a lazy and lingering way; garp means to stare; to mardle is to gossip or chatter. Jiffling is fidgeting; gimbling is sniggering; dudder is to shiver or shake; slummock is an awkward or gawky person; swallacking means sweltering; finnicky is fussy; stingy means mean or miserly. Something on the huh is out of alignment; nonny meant to play the fool but among courting couples it was used to describe the fondling and toying of sweethearts; lollop is to saunter or lounge about; jiggs are the dregs or sediment in the bottom of a pot or bottle; nabble is to gnaw - mice nibble, rats and rabbits nabble; nabbity means short in stature; rare means extraordinary; bread is chaddy when it still has fragments of straw or husks or gritty particles in it; rile means to stir up water in a puddle to make it muddy, hence to vex or annoy.

Here are a couple of jokes to give a flavour of rural humour from a time when the pace of life was slower. Back in the days when cars were not so many, a shiny new open-topped sports car pulled up at a crossroads where an old chap was sitting on a stile contentedly pulling on his pipe. 'Excuse me,' said a posh voice, 'does this road go to Ludham?' The old countryman paused, pulled the pipe from his mouth and looked at the young driver. 'Well now, bor,' said he, 'I've lived here man an' boy for 70 year and tha's never moved yit!'

Two brothers, Charlie and George were helping out on the farm. Charlie, who was a bit accident-prone, fell off the stack and knocked himself out. They sent a boy for the doctor. 'Is he dead?' asked George when the medical man arrived. The doctor examined Charlie and looked up at George. 'Well,

George,' he said in sonorous tones, 'he may be.' At that very moment Charlie came round and heard the doctor's words. 'I ain't dead yet!' he protested. 'Shut you up, bor,' snapped George, 'doctor here knows best.'

Index

Index

Index